D0679311

Exchange-Rate
Instability

This book was set in Palatino by Achorn Graphic Services and printed and bound by Halliday Lithograph in the United States of America.

Library of Congress Cataloging-in-Publication Data

Krugman, Paul R.
  Exchange-rate instability/Paul R. Krugman.

    p. cm.—(The Lionel Robbins lectures)
  Bibliography: p.
  Includes index.
  ISBN 0-262-11140-3
  1. Foreign exchange. 2. International economic integration.
  I. Title. II. Series.
  HG3851.K73   1989   88-17440
  332.4'5–dc19   CIP

Contents

Foreword

One of the most important issues facing the world today is the future of the exchange-rate system. Around 1980 over a million British jobs were lost as a result of an overvalued pound, and a few years later the same happened in America because of an overvalued dollar. These experiences of misalignment astonished those who had hoped that misalignment would be a thing of the past once the world moved to floating exchange rates. They showed the need for a radical reappraisal of the international mechanism for setting exchange rates.

I was therefore delighted when Paul Krugman agreed to give the third annual series of Lionel Robbins Memorial Lectures and to give them on this subject. He is not only one of the world's leading international economists but is equally at home on the monetary and the real side. Thus his lectures are based on a depth of microeconomic understanding which is quite rare in discussions of this subject.

In his first lecture he sets the scene. He offers a new way of understanding why changes in exchange rates may often be necessary: International markets for goods and services are still imperfectly integrated, with most large countries buying at least two-thirds of what they produce. Hence, if a country has a current-account deficit, it cannot cure this simply by cutting spending unless it wants to throw its own workers out of work. It has to make its goods cheaper.

However, in his second lecture Krugman points out that, because of recent exchange-rate turbulence, exchange-rate changes now have less immediate impact on trade imbalances than they used to. For a firm will not necessarily enter a foreign market even if it would do so at the existing rate if it knew the rate would continue. Its entry decision is not unlike the decision to exercise an option to buy a stock. You do not exercise the stock option the moment the purchase becomes profitable, because it may become more profitable. Likewise, a firm enters a foreign market only after the path of the exchange rate has indicated a sufficient level of expected profit. Thus, if exchange rates are volatile, exchange-rate adjustment is less effective at balancing the current account, and this in turn encourages further volatility. Krugman's analysis here is not only original but intensely relevant to the problem of evaluating the "equilibrium" value of a currency.

In his third lecture, Krugman turns to the future of the exchange-rate regime. He makes two key points: First, it is difficult, especially after recent turbulence, to know what is the equilibrium value of each currency. But, second, wide fluctuations in real exchange rates are extremely destructive. Krugman therefore advocates a very gradual return to a fixed-exchange-rate system, with a long initial period in which there is an extremely wide range of target rates.

The book is as important to policy makers as it is to scholars. It is written in the same vigorous style in which the lectures were delivered. The Lionel Robbins Memorial Trust is extremely grateful to Paul Krugman for this splendid contribution to a key debate.

Richard Layard

Exchange-Rate
Instability

1

The Case for Exchange-Rate Flexibility

As you may imagine, the London School of Economics, in addition to offering me the immense privilege of giving these lectures, is also generous enough to offer an honorarium denominated in sterling. From the time that I was first invited to give the lectures, early in the autumn of 1987, until the time that I wrote the lectures in their first draft, the value to me of that honorarium rose by 15 percent. Unfortunately, by the time I gave the lectures a few weeks later, the honorarium's value had declined by 6 percent. My reason for bringing this up is not to complain that my expected affluence has been on a roller coaster, though I admit to finding it a bit disconcerting. Instead, I mention it simply to remind you all what remarkable times we live in. We are now accustomed to experiencing monthly, or even daily, exchange-rate changes that would once have been regarded as major if they had taken place over the course of years. Never before has there been such extraordinary instability of exchange rates in the absence of very high inflation.

Let me take a moment to emphasize how unprecedented the scale of recent exchange-rate instability has been. Compare the recent fluctuations of the dollar with the great monetary events that used to make up our textbook cases. There was Britain's return to gold in the 1920s, which according to Keynes led to an overvaluation of—believe it or not—about 10 percent! There was the 1967 devaluation of sterling—a bitterly disputed, long-resisted move in which, after years of procrastination and attempts to find alternatives, the government finally agreed to allow a 14 percent reduction in the value of the currency. There was the breakup of the Bretton Woods system, in which the United States used heavy-handed political pressure and eventually an illegal tariff to force its trading partners to agree to a 10 percent devaluation. Now look at recent events. From February 1985 to January 1988 the dollar prices of the yen and the mark both rose by 110 percent. From August 1, 1987, to January 1, 1988, the dollar fell against both the yen and the ecu by 16 percent—more than the devaluation of sterling in 1967.

The subject of these three lectures is the instability of exchange rates in the 1980s: what purpose it may serve, why it happens, and what to do about it. In addressing the problem of exchange-rate instability, I have been offered the great privilege of a lecture format, in which the usual rules of careful analysis and rigorous evidence are partially waived. I intend to take full advantage of this privilege by being informal and speculative, by presenting hypothetical and sometimes incompletely formalized theories, and by presenting suggestive rather than conclusive evidence. What you will get here is one economist's view of how the present-day exchange-rate system works. It is a view that I believe is right, that I hope is persuasive, and that in any case I will do my best to make sound controversial.

These lectures will touch on a number of topics within the general question of exchange-rate instability, but I like to imagine that the various ideas I will offer have a common theme: the *imperfect integration* of the world economy. "Imperfect integration" is a double entendre intended to convey two sorts of imperfectness in the way national economies are linked to one another. First, there is the imperfect or limited extent to which countries *are* linked economically. That is, we do not live in a world in which all goods, services, and factors of production move freely across national boundaries; nor are we rapidly becoming such a world, despite some of the rhetoric to which international economists (and others) are susceptible. Second, the integration that we do have doesn't always work as well as we might imagine or hope. International flows of goods and factors of production often do not behave in the smooth, efficient ways that economists often like to suppose. Instead, international markets are imperfectly competitive, characterized by imperfect information, and in some cases demonstrably inefficient.

Why is this important? I will argue in these lectures that the imperfect integration of the world economy is both a cause and an effect of the instability of exchange rates. We could not have the kind of exchange-rate instability we have seen in recent years if the world economy were the kind of tightly integrated system that many economists imagine it to be; and the instability of exchange rates has, in ways that I will attempt to explain later, reduced further the degree of integration. It is also true that an imperfectly integrated world economy poses special problems for policy. You might imagine that the way an imperfectly integrated economy works is somewhere between the way a closed economy would work and the way a perfectly integrated economy would work, but unfortunately that is not the case. Imperfect integration, I will argue, is like imperfect competition: an oligopoly is not an average of a monopoly and a competitive market, and the United States is not an average of an autarky and a city-state. Or, if you prefer your analogies from outside of economics, the study of imperfect integration stands in relation to the polar cases of perfect and zero integration the way that fluid dynamics stands in relation to perfect gases and rigid bodies.

In particular, understanding the imperfectness of international integration, in both its senses, is crucial to our ability to make reasonable policies in a world of fluctuating exchange rates. And indeed I will focus each of these three lectures on a particular question concerning exchange rates. The present lecture will be concerned with the reasons why exchange rates need to change, the second one with the reasons why exchange-rate changes don't seem to matter much anymore, and the third with why exchange rates have misbehaved so badly.

Now, there would not be much point in emphasizing the imperfectness of the world economy's integration if there

were not people arguing on the other side. To put it another way, every good polemic needs a straw man. Fortu-
nately for the interest of these lectures, if not for the world,
there are indeed influential voices on the other side. In
recent years the influence of Ronald McKinnon, Robert
Mundell, and other "global monetarists" has been growing. These economists argue that the insights gained from
simple models of a perfectly integrated world economy
provide a valid basis for policy. The reason for the influence of the global monetarists is clear: Everyone now
knows that the world economy is integrated in important
ways, and perfect integration is a lot easier to explain to
politicians and journalists than imperfect integration. The
global monetarists are always proposing simple stories and
simple policies—purchasing-power parity, a return to the
gold standard—while their opponents are always trying to
explain the difficulties and complexities of the world. It is
hard to explain why purchasing-power parity is only a
useful indicator and not the final word on exchange rates,
why accounting identities are not the same as theories of
behavior, or why any international monetary system is a
compromise between competing objectives rather than the
exactly right solution that absolves governments from the
need to make judgments and decisions.

Along with my discussion of how I believe the floating-
exchange-rate system operates, then, I will be taking occasional sideswipes at the international monetarists, with the
particular aim of doing my best to discredit their mislead-
ing simplicities. As a first step, however, I want to take
time out from my polemic to examine briefly some of the

dimensions of international integration, with particular emphasis on its limits.

The Extent and Trend of International Integration

Someone once wrote that in the story of civilization as told by American historians, the middle class is always rising. Similarly, it seems that in the accounts of the world economy that appear in the media and in popular books, global integration is always increasing. In the postwar period, it is not hard to see how that impression might emerge. From 1950 until about 1980, global integration really was increasing steadily in most dimensions. Trade flows grew twice as rapidly as incomes, capital flows grew from insignificance to considerable importance, and multinational firms extended their operations. By the 1980s it became a commonplace that there is a "megatrend" toward ever greater internationalization, driven by technologies that abolish distance and make the distinction among national economies increasingly irrelevant.

What I want to do briefly here is throw some cold water on that idea. International integration has of course increased greatly since 1950. However, much of the growth was a recovery from an artificially low base; in some important respects the world economy is arguably less well integrated now than it was on the eve of the First World War. Furthermore, the growth of integration has left national economies quite distinct in several ways that are crucial for policy, and this does not appear likely to change anytime soon.

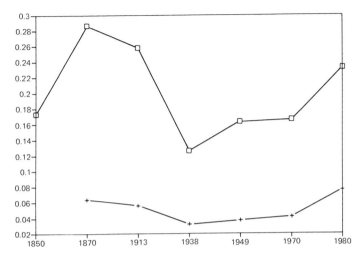

Figure 1.1
Shares of trade in gross national product. □ : United Kingdom;
+ : United States.

As a first, crude indicator of international integration, let us look at the relationship between trade and national income. Figure 1.1 shows the shares of trade—the average of exports and imports—in national income for the United States and the United Kingdom over a number of time periods reaching back to the nineteenth century. It is clear from the figure that extensive trade is nothing new. Aircraft and supertankers are nice additions to the technology of trade, but they have only made the already low costs of international transport still lower. The decisive inventions for international integration were steamships and railroads. The reason that large-scale international trade seems to have emerged only in the postwar period is the extraordinary decline in world trade during the interwar and war years. The proximate reasons for this decline are no mystery; political restriction of trade through tariffs, quotas, and exchange controls reduced trade far below the levels that were technologically feasible. The rapid growth of trade in the postwar period only brought world trade as a share of world product up to its 1913 levels around 1970—that is, the period of most rapidly growing trade was not a product of some immutable technological logic, but a recovery as the political barriers that had inhibited trade were brought down. What the technology of transportation and communication gives, governments can easily take away.

Now, it is true that since 1970 trade has risen to unprecedented levels. All the innovations in transportation and communication since 1913 must be worth something, after all. However, the United States is not now, and very likely will never be, as open to trade as Great Britain has been since the middle of the nineteenth century. Thus, the idea that the growing integration of the world economy has somehow brought us into a wholly new era shows a lack of historical sense.

Moreover, there is one important respect in which the trade of 1988, although larger in volume than the trade of 1913 relative to national income, does less to integrate national economies: Modern trade imposes less commonality on price-level movements than the trade of 75 years ago.

Some of this is structural; both the structure of trade and the structure of economies have changed in ways that reduce the extent of international price linkages. In 1913 most trade was in relatively homogeneous commodities, for which arbitrage determined a world price. Thus, a rise in the price of wheat in Canada was equally reflected in a rise in the price of wheat imported to the United Kingdom. Further, even the advanced nations of the time were primarily goods-producing economies in which the price of raw materials was a large part of costs. Thus, a rise in prices in the world at large would raise a country's import prices, pull up the prices of that country's tradable production, and thereby communicate itself to the domestic price level to a greater degree than the share of trade alone would indicate.

By contrast, in the 1980s most of the trade of advanced countries is in manufactured goods—typically in differentiated products that do not behave like commodities. Goods manufactured in the United States are not auctioned off at prices that are closely affected by the prices of competing goods manufactured abroad; they are instead sold by price-setting firms that are quite resistant to changing their prices in domestic currency. More surprisingly still, even import prices tend to be sticky in the currency of the importing country. There is a remarkable degree of "pricing to market"; for example, many European firms keep their dollar prices of exports to the United States stable despite large swings in their dollar costs when the exchange rate changes. And, in any case, the share of services (primarily nontradable products, such as retail trade) is larger in the economies of the 1980s than in those of the teens, so the range of goods whose prices could be directly affected by international competition is smaller.

In the next lecture I will argue that the structural sources of a decline in the international linkage of prices have been reinforced by a special kind of inertia arising from the volatility of exchange rates. In a world of highly uncertain and erratic exchange rates, firms have an incentive to adopt a "wait and see" attitude toward both trading and pricing decisions—they are cautious about exporting on the basis of a favorable cost position, and tenacious in hanging onto export markets even in the face of unfavorable costs. The result has been a startling delinking of prices of identical commodities in different countries.

The upshot is that international considerations may today play *less* of a role in determining prices in Britain and (especially) the United States than they did in the early years of the century (though they play more of a role than in the 1940s).

There are some other respects in which it is unambiguous that today's markets are less well integrated than those of Edwardian times. The international capital flows of the recent past were minor in comparison with the great flows of the prewar era; we now think of a U.S. current-account deficit of 4 percent of the GNP for a few years as a massive aberration, whereas Britain ran a surplus that exceeded 5 percent of GNP for four decades, and Canada ran a deficit of 13 percent of GNP in 1910–1913. International labor movement in today's world of restricted migration and regulated employment is far less important than the vast flows that populated the zones of recent settlement between 1870 and 1920. I will discuss capital markets in the third lecture; suffice it to say now that international capital markets are imperfectly integrated both in the sense that there is less integration than one might expect and in the sense that these markets have not functioned at all efficiently.

However, I don't want to go too far in debunking. It remains true that the shares of imports and exports in the income of advanced countries are, on the whole, higher now than they have ever been before. What I want to argue next is that not enough integration has been achieved to change two fundamental facts:

1. *Residents of each country have a much higher marginal propensity to spend on the goods they themselves produce than do residents of other countries.*

2. *The prices of each country's labor and goods are sticky in domestic currency.*

The importance of these two facts will become apparent shortly; first I want to establish them.

In addressing my first fact, I am going to focus on the case of the United States—partly because I know the case of my own country best, partly because it is a case that has some interest for us all, and partly because this is, after all, a polemic, and the United States, being less open than any other advanced country, lets me make my case most strongly.

When the residents of the United States raise their expenditure by $1 billion, how much of that increase (other things being equal) will fall on foreign goods?

Tautologically, the answer may be regarded as the product of two terms: the share of imports in expenditure and the elasticity of imports with respect to expenditure. Let us look at the facts for the first and poll the econometricians for the second.

First, let us ask what share of U.S. expenditure falls on foreign goods. You might be inclined to answer with the share of imports in gross national product, or in GNP plus the trade deficit (to take account of the fact that expenditure currently exceeds income)—that is, about 11 percent. This is not a very large number in view of the alarms being raised about international competition in the United States, but it is in any case the wrong number; it is too large by perhaps a factor of 2. On average, U.S. residents probably spend only 5 or 6 percent of their income on imports. The reason is that about half of U.S. imports are intermediate goods. The spending on these goods is presumably related to U.S. output rather than to expenditure, and this makes an important difference.

Next, we poll the econometricians for an elasticity. Import demand is generally estimated to rise more than proportionally to whatever activity variable the econometrician puts in, for fairly obvious reasons: Goods, which are traded more than services, respond more to cyclical fluctuations in spending, and capacity constraints cause some of an increase in demand to spill over into imports. However, the typical elasticity of imports with respect to spending or income is usually around 2 and rarely more than 3. Putting these facts together, we find that a generous estimate of the share of a marginal dollar spent on imports will still be less than 20 cents. Taking a round number, then, lets us suppose that U.S. residents spend 80 percent of a marginal dollar on U.S. goods. What about foreign residents?

The United States is less than a third of the world market economy. Thus, even in normal times, when U.S. trade is roughly balanced, U.S. exports constitute only about 5 percent of the income of the rest of the world, and less of foreigners' final expenditure. A generous estimate might be that foreign residents will spend 10 cents of a marginal dollar on U.S. goods.

Thus, a minimal estimate is that U.S. residents spend 8 times as high a share of a marginal increase in spending on U.S. goods as foreigners. This disparity is, no doubt, smaller than it ever was; however, in an important sense we are still closer to a world in which all of a spending shift falls on domestic goods than to one in which spending is fully internationalized.

Now let us turn to the second point: Prices and wages are sticky in domestic currency. This is both a market imperfection and a kind of imperfect integration. If markets were perfect, of course, wages and prices would move continuously and instantly to clear markets. Even if prices were not totally flexible, however, one could imagine a world in which residents of each country regarded themselves as part of a world economy, with national boundaries making little difference, and in which workers and firms therefore tried to set prices and wages in such a way that they would be indexed against exchange-rate changes (as actually happens in "dollarized" economies like that of Israel a few years back). In such a world, exchange rates would have little real significance, since a change in the nominal exchange rate would simply produce some combination of inflation in the depreciating country and deflation in the appreciating country. The neutrality of nominal exchange rates is a key theme of the global monetarists, sometimes expressed in the slogan that the exchange rate is the relative price of two moneys, *not* the relative price of two goods or two kinds of labor.

Well, let us take a look at the facts. Figure 1.2 plots the U.S. nominal exchange rate (actually, an average index against other OECD countries) versus an index of U.S. relative unit labor costs (using the same weights). Guess what? The exchange rate *is* the relative price of two kinds of labor.

Figure 1.3 does the same for prices, comparing the nominal dollar with the price of U.S. exports relative to the export prices of the rest of the OECD. It turns out that the exchange rate is the relative price of two goods also.

Why is this true? I don't want to take a long detour into macroeconomics here, but the basic point seems perfectly clear. Whether because of menu costs or because of bounded rationality, firms do not constantly change their

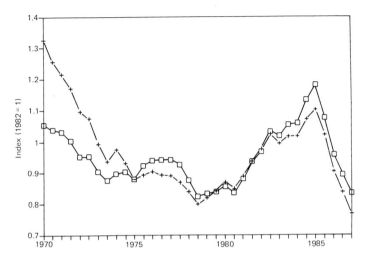

Figure 1.2
Nominal versus real exchange rate. □ : exchange rate; + : relative unit labor cost.

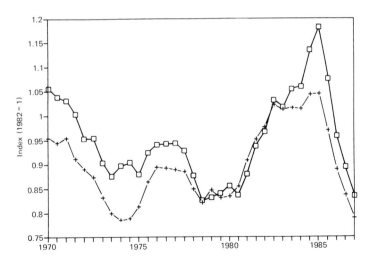

Figure 1.3
Nominal versus real exchange rate. □ : exchange rate; + : relative price.

prices and their wage offers in response to changes in demand, nor do they index their prices optimally. Instead, they fix prices in nominal terms for fairly long periods, and the overlapping pricing decisions of thousands of price setters create substantial inertia in the overall level of wages and prices.

The important addendum for international economics is that when prices are set in nominal terms, they are set in terms of domestic currency. In principle, this needn't happen. Prices in Germany could be set in dollars, or prices in Italy in ecu; the medium of exchange and the unit of account functions of money can be, and sometimes are, separated. In advanced countries, however, prices are sufficiently predictable that there is no need to turn to a foreign currency for a usable standard (in contrast with the situation in hyperinflation countries). And the fact is that domestic currency has a much more predictable purchasing power for residents of every advanced country than any foreign currency—even for imports. So the end result is that prices and wages are sticky in each nation in terms of that country's own currency.

This seems straightforward enough. I would leave the subject here and go on to policy issues, except that the state of debate in contemporary economics doesn't let me. To me, the *prima facie* case that prices are sticky is overwhelming, and the implied imperfection of markets is not particularly disturbing. For many of my colleagues, however, continuous market clearing and the absence of any money illusion are fundamental tenets, and this obliges them to explain away the appearance of price inflexibility as some kind of optical illusion. In particular, one now often hears the argument that the kind of evidence I have presented in figures 1.2 and 1.3 has got the causation backwards—that what really happens is that real exchange rates are moving around for real reasons, and the attempt of monetary authorities to stabilize domestic price levels creates the correlation between real and nominal rates.

At one level, this argument can be dismissed as silly. What were the real shocks that raised the equilibrium relative price of U.S. labor by 15 percent from the second quarter of 1984 to the first quarter of 1985, then drove it down by 22 percent over the following year? However, ridicule doesn't seem to work here. Perhaps I can also offer a more persuasive piece of evidence. Suppose that you thought that real exchange rates were a real phenomenon, and that they were not affected by nominal rates. Then there would be no particular reason why a change in the exchange-rate regime should alter the behavior of real exchange rates. In particular, one would expect real exchange rates to be no more variable under floating rates than under fixed rates.

Figure 1.4 (which is borrowed from Rudiger Dornbusch and Alberto Giovannini) shows monthly changes in the real exchange rate (using wholesale prices as deflators) between the United States and the Federal Republic of Germany from 1960 to 1986. The first half of this graph shows the experience under fixed rates, the second half the experience under floating rates. Need I say more? The variance

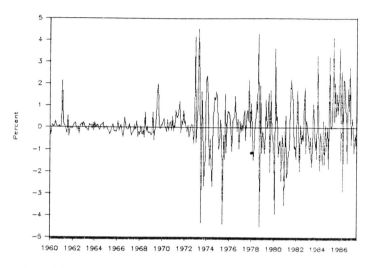

Figure 1.4
Monthly changes in real exchange rate between the United States and
the Federal Republic of Germany, 1960–1986.

of monthly changes in the real exchange rate was 15 times
as large in the second half of the sample as in the first.

Now, I suppose that a complete "true believer" might argue at this point for the endogeneity of exchange-rate re-
gimes themselves. The argument would run as follows:
The structure of the real economy changed in the early
1970s in a way that vastly increased the equilibrium volatility of relative prices; and central banks, unconsciously appreciating this change, altered the exchange regime. To
answer this, I suppose that we can go to even further
lengths. For example, Alan Stockman and Marianne Baxter
of the University of Rochester have found that before the
Republic of Ireland joined the European Monetary System,
its real exchange rate was more closely correlated with that

of the United Kingdom than with that of Germany; after Ireland joined, it became more correlated with Germany than with the U.K. If you believe that this represents a real change unconnected to the change in exchange arrangements, I wash my hands of your case and advise that you consult a specialist.

Realistically, then, we know as surely as we know anything in economics that price levels are sticky in domestic currency. Next I will argue that the combination of the two imperfections of international integration that has now been documented—the domestic bias of each country's spending, and the stickiness of prices in domestic currency—has direct implications for exchange-rate policy.

The Case for Changing the Exchange Rate

In 1987 the United States ran a current-account deficit of about $160 billion. It is an accounting identity that the difference between exports and imports is equal to the difference between national income and expenditure, which in turn is equal to the difference between national saving and investment. As it happens, the unprecedented U.S. deficit had as its counterpart not an unusually high level of investment but the lowest level of national savings since the depths of the Depression—largely, though not wholly, because the federal government has been engaging in massive dissaving. One expects and hopes that, one way or another, U.S. saving will rise in the near future to a more normal level, and that when it does the U.S. trade position will also move toward a more normal level—say, zero.

What would be the appropriate exchange-rate policy to accompany this hoped-for adjustment? The conventional wisdom is that adjustment of world payments balances requires exchange-rate adjustments: depreciation by deficit countries and appreciation by surplus countries. Such conventional wisdom underlay the Plaza Accord and the general approval with which the initial fall of the dollar was greeted. More and more, however, one now hears this conventional wisdom challenged, especially by the global monetarists. Indeed, we have now begun to see the development of a new conventional wisdom (a neoconventional wisdom?) that argues that exchange rates should be set on the basis of criteria other than balance-of-payments adjustment, and that balance-of-payments adjustment, if it is a concern of policy at all, should be handled through fiscal measures. This point of view has become the official party line at the *Wall Street Journal* and has percolated into the discourse of real-world policymakers—notably, I am sorry to say, the UK's Chancellor Lawson.

The reason for this influence is that the neoconventional wisdom offers a seductive simplicity that can be made to seem very plausible. The trade balance is, by definition, equal to the difference between saving and investment—and therefore, say McKinnon, Mundell, and the *Wall Street Journal*, the exchange rate has nothing to do with it. Dollar depreciation, on this view, doesn't help reduce the U.S. trade deficit; all it does is produce inflation in the U.S. and deflation abroad. What we should do, therefore, is fix the dollar now at a level consistent with some estimate of purchasing-power parity, which means currently at a level far above present parities, and peg it there forever. McKinnon wants us to move thereafter to a global monetary target (in effect, a paper simulation of a gold standard); Mundell wants us to move back to a true gold standard.

It is easy to see where this new conventional wisdom comes from. It would be precisely right if we lived in a perfectly integrated world, where residents of each country spent their income the same way, and where price levels in every country were perfectly flexible—or at least if there were no special inflexibility of prices in terms of domestic currency. Unfortunately, we do not live in such a world. As we have just seen, the world is very imperfectly integrated in vital ways: Residents of different countries spend their incomes very differently, and prices are sticky in domestic currency. Imagining a perfectly integrated world is a useful exercise for thinking about some aspects of international economics, but proposing that we make policy as if we actually lived in such a world is a prescription for disaster.

Suppose that the OECD countries were to attempt to narrow their payments imbalances while keeping both exchange rates and domestic price levels stable. Suppose, in particular, that the United States were to take the necessary actions to reduce its spending by $100 billion, while the rest of the OECD were to increase its spending by the same amount—for there is no question that such a redistribution of expenditures is a necessary condition for correcting the imbalance in payments. The global monetarists would have us believe that that is the end of the story;

Table 1.1
Reducing a trade imbalance.

	Spending on U.S. products	Spending on RoW products[a]
Case A		
U.S. spending −100	U.S.: −80	U.S.: −20
RoW spending +100	RoW: +10	RoW: +90
Case B		
U.S. spending −100	U.S.: −80	U.S.: −20
RoW spending +800	RoW: +80	RoW: +720

a. RoW: rest of world

however, it isn't, as one can immediately see by looking at table 1.1 (for which I am indebted to Sam Brittan).

Case A in table 1.1 shows what happens, all else equal, if U.S. spending falls by $100 billion and the rest of the world's spending rises by the same amount. The key point is that, as I argued above, U.S. residents have a much higher marginal propensity to spend on U.S. goods than RoW residents. When U.S. spending falls by $100 billion, U.S. spending on imports falls by only $20 billion, while domestic demand for U.S. goods falls by $80 billion. The increase in RoW spending provides a new source of demand for U.S. exports, but not nearly enough; out of the $100 billion rise in RoW spending, only $10 billion falls on U.S. products. The result, then, is a $70 billion excess supply of U.S. goods and a $70 billion excess demand for RoW goods.

How can the redistribution of world expenditures be made effective? Somehow the world needs to be persuaded to *switch* $70 billion of spending from RoW goods to U.S. goods. Other than moral exhortation (such as "Buy American" bumper stickers, and the "Buy imports" signs that the Japanese for a while put on shopping carts at Narita Airport), the only nonprotectionist way to do this is to make U.S. goods relatively cheap. That is, we need a real U.S.-against-RoW depreciation.

The reason why this real depreciation is needed is precisely that world markets for goods and services are imperfectly integrated, so that residents of each country have a much higher propensity to spend on their own products than residents of other countries. Thus, the microeconomic fact of an imperfectly integrated world market has the macroeconomic implication that changes in the real exchange rate are an essential part of the process of adjusting the balance of payments.

The key point is the imperfect integration of world markets for *goods and services.* A number of people, McKinnon in particular, have claimed that the alleged fact of integrated *capital* markets allows savings to be transferred from one country to another without changes in relative prices. I am going to raise some doubts about the capital markets in my third lecture, but in any case it should be clear that this argument is fundamentally confused. All that a capital market can do is facilitate the redistribution of spending from one country to another. But the need for relative-price change depends on what is done with the spending—whether 125 yen spent in Japan are spent in the same way as a dollar spent in the United States. This is not a question about financial markets; it is a question about the actual final demands for goods and services. Anyone who imagines the contrary has fallen into financial mysticism.

Because of the imperfect integration of world markets for goods and services, then, current-account adjustment does require adjustment of the real exchange rate. However, it is not necessary that this occur through a nominal depreciation of the dollar. Instead of through a decline in the dollar, we could achieve the same result through a combination of deflation in the United States and inflation abroad. The need for real-exchange-rate adjustment is a case for nominal-exchange-rate flexibility only if relative prices and wages are more easily altered through changes in the exchange rate than through differential movements in the price level. But of course they are. Because there is in fact tremendous inertia to nominal prices (that is, to nominal prices in each country's currency), it is vastly easier to reduce the relative price of U.S. labor and output via a dollar depreciation than to do so via U.S. deflation. The overwhelming evidence for sticky nominal prices in domestic currency is therefore the final link in the argument in favor of allowing nominal depreciation by deficit countries.

Let me once again belabor the point, in a way that may help clarify the logic of currency depreciation as an adjustment tool. Suppose that, as part of a world balance-of-payments adjustment, it is necessary for the United States to reduce its wages relative to those of other nations by 30 percent. Try to imagine doing this without a decline in the dollar. Thirty percent is a huge wage cut, and an individual wage earner or a union would resist it bitterly. Yet a 30 percent cut in wages for all U.S. workers would by no means involve a 30 percent cut in real wages; since in our imperfectly integrated world the bulk of what each U.S. worker consumes is produced by other U.S. workers, the real wage cut implied would be more like 3 percent. This doesn't sound like all that much; and if every worker understood that other workers' wages would be cut at the same time as his own, and that these lower wage costs would be reflected in lower prices, one might imagine a coordinated reduction in wages that could take place quickly and almost painlessly. Unfortunately, that's not the way the world works; the sluggishness of pricing at the individual-firm level, combined with the problem of overlapping and uncoordinated price setting, means that a 30-percent wage reduction could be achieved, if at all, only via a huge and protracted recession.

What a currency depreciation does is solve the coordination problem. When the dollar falls against the yen and the ecu, all U.S. wages fall together and simultaneously, with no need for anyone to cut a nominal wage. Of course, if wages were indexed to the exchange rate, or to the general price level with a quick pass-through of exchange rates into prices, a dollar depreciation would immediately be reflected in massive inflation. However, though this may happen in near-hyperinflation economies, it just doesn't happen in advanced economies with moderate to low inflation. And a large part of the reason it doesn't happen is the same reason that changes in the real exchange rate are necessary in the first place: With the bulk of domestic expenditure going to domestic goods, price setters do not have a strong incentive to set prices in anything other than domestic currency.

We have gone, then, from the observation that we still live in a world of rather limited international integration to a clear policy case for exchange-rate flexibility. That is a general point, not a specific one about current events. Since the topicality of this view makes it controversial, however, I want to cover myself by briefly discussing a few caveats with regard to the analysis I have presented.

Three Caveats

• Differences in marginal spending patterns would not require large changes in the real exchange rate if goods produced in different countries were very close substitutes, so that a small shift in relative prices would lead to large changes in the composition of demand. Therefore, I really need to tie up loose ends with an argument that goods from different countries are not excessively close substitutes. This should be obvious, however. At a gross level, the huge swings in relative wages and prices shown in figures 1.2 and 1.3 would not have been possible in a world where goods produced in different countries were close substitutes. In fact, it is hard to understand how they are possible even in a world where goods are highly imperfect substitutes—a subject I will address in the second lecture. Anyway, this casual evidence may be supplemented by the econometric literature on trade, which uniformly finds rather low price elasticities (on the order of 1–2).

• A more serious point is that while emphasizing the lack of perfect integration among national economies I have oversimplified the national economies themselves, in effect treating the United States as if it were producing only one good. In fact, exchange-rate changes are of course associated with important changes in the relative prices of tradables and nontradables produced by each country. This is another issue that I will address at greater length tomorrow. The important point now is that it does not affect the basic conclusion that adjusting the balance of payments requires large changes in relative national price levels on average and (even more important) large changes in relative national wage rates. Even with exchange-rate adjustment some problems may arise because of difficulties in adjusting relative prices within a country, but these are surely minor in comparison with the problems of getting the necessary overall price adjustment without changing the exchange rate.

• The main practical point that needs to be mentioned concerns the role of growth in the surplus countries. In case A of table 1.1, it is assumed that the fall in U.S. expenditure is matched by only an equal rise in RoW expenditure. Many in the United States have argued, however, that growth in surplus countries—which means a rise in RoW expenditure over and above the fall in U.S. expenditure, whether they realize it or not—should take the place of exchange-rate adjustment. This point is correct conceptually, but there just isn't much in it as a practical matter. Let us return to case B of table 1.1 to see why.

How much would foreign expenditure have to rise in order to allow the United States to cut its expenditure by $100 billion and convert all of that cut into a trade-balance improvement without the need for a real depreciation to induce a switch of expenditure to U.S. goods? The answer is shown by case B. Since the fall in U.S. expenditure reduces the demand for U.S. goods by $80 billion, and we are assuming that only 10 percent of a marginal increase in RoW spending falls on U.S. goods, expenditure in the rest of the world must rise by $800 billion. In this way the total spending on U.S. goods is left unchanged, with the decline in domestic demand offset by an equal increase in export demand.

Unfortunately, there is a side consequence: The total expenditure on RoW goods rises by $700 billion—the $720 billion increase in domestic demand minus the $20 billion fall in U.S. imports. Thus, the alternative to U.S. depreciation offered here will work only if there is at least $700 billion of usable excess capacity in the rest of the world. At current exchange rates, the gross national products of market economies outside the United States amount to about $9 trillion, so this means that improving the United States' trade position by $100 billion using foreign growth as an alternative to real depreciation would require that we find room for an increase of almost 8 percent in the rest of the world's GNP. If we were to try to deal with the whole U.S. trade deficit in this way, the foreign growth would have to be more like 12 percent.

The problem should be immediately obvious: There isn't that much excess capacity in the surplus countries. Indeed, the International Monetary Fund has estimated that none of the industrial countries with current-account surpluses has a usable excess capacity of more than 2 percent of GNP. You may not believe that estimate, but whether you or I believe it is not the important point. What matters is what the policymakers in the surplus countries believe, and the fact is that they (in particular, the authorities in Germany) regard themselves as having little room for expansion. Thus, the possibility of substituting growth in surplus countries for adjustment of the real exchange rate, while correct in principle, is only a minor issue in the current context.

By the way, I am not arguing against German expansion, or even arguing that faster growth in Europe and Japan is not an important issue. It is—but not for the U.S. trade deficit. And the repeated suggestions that the United States would be willing to trade a higher dollar for a little bit of German or Japanese stimulus show that policymakers are just not doing their arithmetic (not for the first time).

Where We Are Now

I began this lecture by pointing out that, despite the increase in some aspects of international integration since 1950, the integration of the world economy is still highly imperfect. I hope that I have documented the imperfect integration of goods markets and the continuing stickiness of each country's prices in domestic currency to everyone's satisfaction. And I have shown with what I believe is iron-clad logic that the combination of imperfectly integrated goods markets and sticky prices creates a compelling argument for exchange-rate adjustment in the face of international imbalances of payments.

There is, however, a problem with making this argument in the late 1980s: exchange-rate changes have not seemed to work very well lately. The most obvious problem is the disappointing slowness with which the U.S. trade deficit responded to the dollar decline that began in 1985, but the problem actually began even earlier. Throughout the rise and fall of the dollar in the 1980s, there has been a growing slippage in the gears between the exchange rate and the real world of international trade flows and prices. This slippage was already pronounced during the dollar's rise, and has become a source of serious puzzlement and concern as the dollar has fallen. If international trade were an automobile and exchange rates its transmission, I would say that we need a new clutch.

What is going on here? You won't be surprised to hear me say once again that we need to think about the problem in terms of the imperfect integration of the world economy—which, I am going to argue, has in an important sense become still more imperfect because of the volatility of exchange rates. Why don't exchange rates seem to matter very much? That will be the subject of the next lecture.

Appendix: The Trade Balance and the Real Exchange Rate

As I stressed in the first lecture, the fact that the trade deficit is equal to the excess of spending over income does not mean that trade balances can be altered without changes in relative prices. This point is understood surprisingly poorly, even by some highly trained economists—perhaps because we have become so concerned with working out sophisticated intertemporal models that we have lost sight of the partial relationships that underlie them. In any case, I find it useful to buttress the intuitive explanation with a simple algebraic model. The model presented here (first presented in Krugman and Baldwin 1987) makes the point in a simple, though not general, way.

Consider a world economy consisting of only the United States and the rest of the world (RoW). Each of these two "countries" produces a single good that is both consumed domestically and exported. Let RoW's output be the numeraire, and define p as the relative price of the U.S. good. Initially, assume full employment, so that the U.S. produces a fixed output y and RoW produces a fixed output, y^*. Leave the determination of expenditure in the background, simply treating U.S. expenditure in terms of its own good as a parameter, a. For the world as a whole, income must equal expenditure. Thus, if a^* is RoW expenditure, measured in terms of the RoW good, it must be true that

$$pa + a^* = py + y^*, \tag{A.1}$$

or

$$a^* = y^* + p(y - a).$$

Now, it is certainly true that, as an accounting identity, the trade balance is equal to the excess of income over expenditure, so that the U.S. trade balance, in terms of the U.S.

good, is simply

$$t = y - a \tag{A.2}$$

(an expression in which the relative price of U.S. goods does not directly appear).

This does not, however, allow us to forget about relative prices. There is still a requirement that the market for U.S. output clear (in which case the market for RoW output clears as well, by Walras's Law). Each country will divide its expenditure between the two goods. For simplicity, make the Cobb-Douglas assumption that expenditure shares are fixed, with the U.S. spending m of its income on imports and $1 - m$ on domestic output and RoW spending m^* on imports and $1 - m^*$ on domestic goods. Then the market-clearing condition can be written as

$$py = (1 - m)pa + m^*a^*, \tag{A.3}$$

or

$$p[y - (1 - m)a] = m^*a^*$$
$$= m^*[y^* + p(y - a)],$$

implying

$$p = m^*y^*/D \tag{A.4}$$

where

$$D = (1 - m)y - (1 - m - m^*)a.$$

The implications of this small model are illustrated in figure A.1, which is much more general than the example. On the horizontal axis is the U.S. level of real expenditure, a, while on the vertical axis is the relative price of U.S.

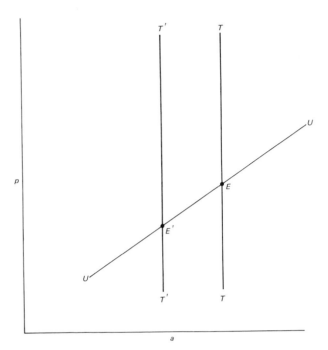

Figure A.1

output, p. The line TT is an *iso-trade-balance* line; that is, it represents a locus of points consistent with some given trade balance in terms of U.S. output. The accounting identity that equates the trade balance to income minus expenditure, regardless of relative prices, is reflected by the fact that TT is vertical. Meanwhile, the line UU represents points of market clearing for U.S. output. It is drawn here with a positive slope, which will be the case if $(1 - m) > m^*$ (that is, if U.S. residents have a higher marginal propensity to spend on U.S. output than RoW residents do). Point E is the equilibrium for a given trade balance.

If the picture is as drawn in figure A.1, a reduction in the U.S. trade deficit will necessarily be accompanied by a decline in the relative price of U.S. output. A reduction of U.S. real expenditure shifts TT inward to $T'T'$; this requires that the equilibrium shift from E to E', which involves a fall in the relative price, p.

Now, there are two circumstances in which this adjustment in the relative price need not take place. One is the case where U.S. and RoW goods are perfect substitutes (that is, where it is effectively a one-good world). The other is the case where spending patterns are identical between countries, so that $1 - m = m^*$. In either case, the effect is to make UU horizontal (figure A.2), so that a reduction in

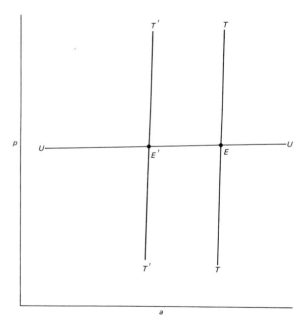

Figure A.2

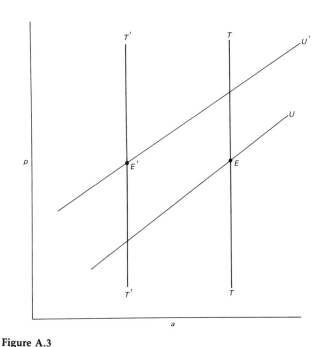

Figure A.3

U.S. expenditure need not be accompanied by a decline in the relative price of what the U.S. produces.

It is also possible for the trade deficit to fall without real depreciation if foreign output expands. From equation A.4, an increase in foreign output, y^*, will shift UU up; thus, if there is excess capacity in the RoW it is possible to have a scenario in which U.S. expenditure falls without any real depreciation (figure A.3).

2   The Delinking of Exchange Rates from Reality

Everyone knows the Sherlock Holmes story in which the crucial clue is the fact that a dog did *not* bark—that is, where the important evidence is what didn't happen, not what did. In this lecture I want to make a similar point about the functioning of the floating-exchange-rate regime. One of the most puzzling, and therefore one of the most important, aspects of the floating rates of the 1980s has been that huge swings in exchange rates have had only muted effects on anything real. Over the past decade we have experienced what must be the largest exchange-rate changes ever to occur in the absence of large inflation differentials. In view of the size of these fluctuations, the remarkable thing is not how much effect exchange-rate changes have had but how little. And behind the puzzle of why exchange rates matter so little is, I will argue, a story about the workings of our imperfect world economy that may be crucially important to our views about exchange-rate policy.

Let us return to my favorite figure from the previous lecture: figure 1.2, which compares the U.S. nominal

exchange rate with its relative unit labor cost in manufacturing. Notice just how enormous the swings have
been. Relative to an average of other industrial countries,
U.S. unit labor costs rose no less than 60 percent from 1980
to their peak in the first half of 1985; then in less than three
years they fully reversed that rise. Or, to be specific, compare the United States with Germany. In 1980 German
wages in manufacturing were about 25 percent higher in
dollars than American wages. At the dollar's peak they
were about 25 percent *lower*. By early 1988 they were once
again about 20 percent higher.

Now imagine that we were to find an economist who has
been snowbound in Pittsburgh, Rochester, or Minneapolis
for the past decade and knows nothing about what has
been happening in the outside world, and that we were to
inform him of the size of these shocks. We may well suppose that he would conclude that, with U.S. costs as far
out of line as they were in early 1985, the American manufacturing sector must surely have collapsed. Conversely,
the sharp decline of U.S. relative unit labor costs since that
peak must surely have devastated the manufacturing sec-
tors of Japan and Western Europe. On seeing the actual
data, he would be shocked, not by how much effect the
gyrations of the dollar have had, but by how little. The
United States has indeed moved into massive trade deficit
in manufacturing; however, the deficit is only 15 percent of
manufacturing value added, and the country's overall
manufacturing output has risen almost as rapidly during
the 1980s as during the 1970s. The decline of the dollar has
indeed cut into the real net exports of manufactured goods

from Japan and Europe, but it has hardly led to wholesale deindustrialization.

Even more amazing is the lack of major impact on inflation. One need not have blind faith in purchasing-power parity to think that large exchange-rate changes should have an inflationary impact on the depreciating countries and a deflationary effect on the appreciators. In the early years of floating rates there was widespread discussion of the concept of "vicious and virtuous circles," which assigned exchange rates the central role in divergent inflation performance among OECD nations. When the dollar was at its peak, those who worried about its eventual fall emphasized the inflationary impact that would follow. Stephen Marris, for example, quite correctly forecast a "hard landing" of the dollar; but he expected this to lead to a hard landing for the economy as well, because the inflationary impact would necessitate contractionary monetary policy.

The fact is, however, that the movements of the dollar have simply not been reflected in or offset by much divergence in inflation. This is implicit in figure 1.2; the fact that the nominal exchange rate and relative unit labor costs have moved almost perfectly in tandem tells us that not much was happening to relative inflation rates. Or simply think about the events. The decline of every other currency against the dollar from 1980 to 1985 did not prevent Japan and Europe from experiencing a steady reduction in domestic inflation rates, which led to essentially stable prices in Germany and Japan. The decline in the dollar has been accompanied by a slight increase in the U.S. inflation rate, but not enough to be regarded as a significant reversal of the victory over inflation won by the 1982 recession, or, at least so far, enough to begin to feed into wage demands.

Over the past few years, and especially since the dollar began declining, we have imperceptibly become accustomed to living in a world in which exchange rates move by huge amounts but the changes have only small effects on anything else. As I emphasized in the first lecture, the exchange-rate changes since the dollar's peak in 1985 dwarf those that were central to great historical disputes. Yet, looking at the domestic performance of the major economies, one sees only marginal impacts from these changes.

In fact, exchange-rate fluctuations of the size we have seen recently are possible only because they have so little effect. If changes in the relative costs of producing manufactured goods in different countries were quickly reflected in changes in the actual locations of production, large swings in the dollar would produce trade-balance changes that would themselves place limits on those swings. If exchange-rate changes were passed through rapidly into domestic prices, the kind of exchange-rate movements we have seen either would lead to massive differences in inflation (which would mean that the large nominal-rate changes would not be matched by comparable changes in real rates) or would be met by nonaccommodating monetary policy (which would again limit the exchange-rate fluctuations). It is only because there seems to be some kind of delinking of exchange rates and the real economy that exchange rates can be as volatile as they have been. That is, *exchange rates can move so much precisely because they seem to matter so little.*

But why do exchange rates matter so little? At least one proximate reason is now clear: that exchange rates do not affect trade flows or aggregate prices as much as one might expect is due in large part to the fact that firms that sell goods to other countries do not change their prices to the importing country as much as one might expect. This phenomenon of "pricing to market" itself needs explanation. As a preliminary step, let us look at some of the evidence on how prices of traded goods have behaved in the 1980s.

Pricing to Market in Practice

This lecture is about dogs that didn't bark, and figure 2.1 illustrates a case of acute canine laryngitis. It compares the real "import" exchange rate of the dollar with the real price of manufactures imports (deflated by the GNP deflator) since the dollar's peak in the first half of 1985. (The "import" exchange rate is a number calculated by the Federal Reserve and supplied to me by William Helkie. It contains ten advanced countries and eight less-developed countries, weighted by their shares in U.S. imports. Its behavior is somewhat different from that of the multilateral, industrial-country indices used elsewhere in these lectures— notably, the dollar fell less by this measure since the peak.) The figure hardly needs discussing. Two years after the dollar began to fall, real import prices were still below their

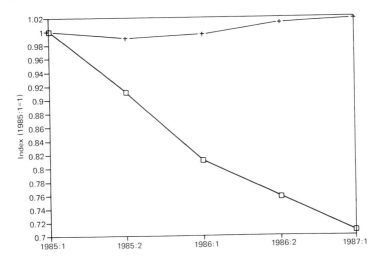

Figure 2.1
Exchange rate versus import prices. □ : real exchange rate; + : real import price.

initial level; even a year later, they had risen by only a derisory fraction of the dollar's decline. No doubt there is another import-price increase just around the corner, so if we focus only on the rate of change the impact of the declining dollar will become increasingly apparent in the months to come. Relative to what anyone might have expected, however, the striking fact is how small and how late the import-price increase has been.

Some sophisticated skeptics might object to the crudity of the comparison I have made here, although I have tried to use a more or less correct exchange-rate index that gives a high weight to Canada and to those less-developed countries whose currencies have not appreciated against the dollar. Also, I will assert that more careful studies, espe-

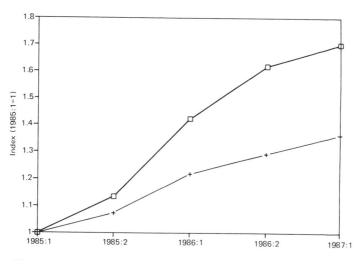

Figure 2.2
Japanese export pricing. □ : dollar costs; + : dollar prices.

cially those by Catherine Mann and Peter Hooper at the
Federal Reserve Board (Mann 1987; Hooper and Mann
1987) confirm that import-price increases have fallen dras-
tically short of what one would have expected given the
change in any reasonable exchange-rate index. Equally, we
can use alternative measures to show that the failure of
U.S. import prices to rise much has as its counterpart a
compression of the margin of prices over costs in exporting
countries. Figure 2.2, which compares Japan's unit labor
costs with its manufactures export prices, both measured
in dollars, shows clearly that Japanese manufacturers have
tried to stabilize their prices in export markets rather than
to keep their prices in line with their costs. Moving from
the aggregate to the very specific, I have looked at the price
of Volvos exported from Sweden to the United States.
From 1985 to 1987, Swedish unit labor costs rose by 70

percent measured in dollars, while the price of Volvos rose only 17 percent. Thus, once again we see a spectacular unwillingness to change export prices when the exchange rates changes.

The stickiness of prices of traded goods in the face of exchange-rate fluctuations has barely touched the competing conventional wisdoms that inform practical discussion in international economics. The policy debate is between the global monetarists, who like to imagine that the whole world produces a single good whose price is equalized by international arbitrage, and the more traditional Keynesian view that nations produce different goods whose relative prices can and indeed must move as part of the process of international adjustment. I argued in the first lecture that the global monetarists' position is foolish and wrong in theory and in practice, and that the Keynesian view is much more realistic. However, we must now admit that international Keynesianism, while more like reality than international monetarism, itself turns out to have a problem: It does not go far enough in rejecting international arbitrage. Not only does the Law of One Price fail to hold at the level of aggregate national price indices, contrary to what many economists and journalists obstinately believe; it doesn't even hold at the level of individual goods. The relative prices of Volvos in the United States and Sweden have fluctuated nearly as much over the past decade as the relative aggregate consumer price indices, adjusted for the exchange rate.

How can this be? Recently a few economists have begun to propose a possible explanation of the sluggish adjustment of both trade prices and trade quantities in response to massive exchange-rate changes. I will call this explanation the *sunk cost model*. It is still a speculative idea, not grounded in solid empirical tests; but it is a good story, and if it is correct it has extremely important implications for economic policy. I will offer here an informal exposition of the sunk cost model, making the best case I can for it and for its implications.

The Sunk Cost Model

The basic idea of the sunk cost model is that trade does not come easily. In the case of the differentiated manufactured goods that make up most of the trade of advanced countries, it is not enough for a firm to offer a high-quality product at a reasonable price and to expect competitive shippers to perform the task of international arbitrage. Instead, a firm that wants to export must invest substantial resources in adapting its product to the foreign market, in developing a marketing and distribution network, and often in creating production capability specially geared to what foreigners will be willing to buy. Anecdotal evidence about Japan's export drive speaks of the years of losses that firms had to be willing to incur in order to penetrate foreign markets, which is a kind of investment akin to the costs a firm must incur to move down the learning curve when adopting a new technology.

Now, the important point about the investment aspect of international trade for my current purposes is that typically the costs of entering a foreign market may be regarded as *sunk* once they have been incurred—that is, a firm cannot easily sell off its assets, visible or invisible. If at some point a firm that has incurred considerable expense to break into a foreign market decides that it cannot profitably continue to sell in that market, it must write off that expense. What the sunk cost model does is point out that this irreversibility of investment can make trade rather unresponsive to the exchange rate—particularly when exchange rates are highly volatile.

The obvious point is the naive one that a firm will be willing to break into a market only if it expects to cover its sunk costs, and that once the costs are sunk it will be willing to stay in a market even if it is able to cover only its variable cost. Thus, even if firms had purely static expectations, always expecting the future to be exactly like the present, there would be for each firm a "range of no change"—a range of the exchange rate over which a firm will continue exporting if it is already doing so but will not be induced to begin exporting if it did not start out in that position.

This simple role of sunk costs can explain why small exchange-rate fluctuations might not have much effect on the pattern of specialization: A movement of a few percent in the relative cost of producing manufactured goods in the United States and in Germany will not make it worthwhile for firms to incur the cost of breaking into a new market, or induce firms already in the market to drop out. That is, it can explain why production of manufactured goods is not totally footloose and not well described by a view of the world economy as driven by arbitrage. However, it is not immediately obvious from the role of sunk costs why trade flows and pricing should be so insensitive to the huge exchange-rate swings we have seen recently, nor is it obvious why trade should appear to be so much less sensitive to exchange-rate fluctuations now than it was in the past. Admittedly, there are probably more customer markets and fewer auction markets in trade now than 75 years ago (a point I emphasized in the first lecture). But the changes since the 1970s have not been dramatic enough to produce the remarkable insensitivity of modern trade to currency fluctuations.

A second level of explanation would stress the fact that firms do not in fact have static expectations. When the dollar was at its peak, most manufacturing firms realized that it could not and would not stay there indefinitely (in this they were more intelligent and reasonable than the financial markets, which completely lost touch with reality). Conversely, many firms have (until recently, at least) reportedly been betting that the weakness of the dollar represents overshooting by the financial markets, and that the dollar will eventually settle at a value somewhere above its current level—for example, for quite a while Japanese firms were reported to have been planning on the basis of 170–180 yen to the dollar, when the actual rate was 150 or higher. To the extent that firms' plans are based on expected exchange rates that lag the actual, we can easily understand a limited response to a swing in the exchange rate: Firms will not enter markets as soon as the returns at the current rate exceed the annualized value of sunk costs if they believe that today's favorable exchange rate is only temporary; they will not abandon a market, even when they cannot cover variable costs, if they view themselves as hanging onto a position that will in the not-too-distant future be profitable once more.

The idea that market responses to exchange rates are limited by regressive expectations is helpful in understanding why the responses to exchange rates have been more limited in the 1980s than in the past. The huge swings of the exchange rate in the 1980s have clearly been more likely to be interpreted as temporary consequences of capital flows or speculative bubbles than past exchange-rate changes. It is probably true that, whereas in the Bretton Woods era devaluations were generally regarded as permanent and elicited rapid reevaluations of firms' strategies, the ups and downs of the floating-rate period have been regarded as temporary aberrations and have, to some extent, been disregarded by firms. The anecdotes are easy to come by. For example, Caterpillar Tractor grimly hung onto its market share in anticipation that the dollar would eventually fall enough to make it competitive again (which it did), and Mercedes-Benz chose not to cut its dollar prices and expand its U.S. sales beyond the luxury market because it did not regard the three-mark dollar as a long-term proposition. When the exchange rate is seen as fluctuating around its long-term value, firms may discount much of what it does in the short term.

There is, however, a third-level explanation, which seems to me to be a much deeper and more profound explanation of the immobility of trade with respect to the exchange rate: that volatility of the exchange rate, even when it is not regarded as resulting from some kind of process that quickly reverts to the mean, encourages firms to adopt a "wait and see" attitude; they become reluctant both to enter new markets and to exit from old ones. This idea is a new one; my exposition of it is based on two recent papers by Avinash Dixit (1987a,b) (though I, of course, take responsibility for the particular interpretation I place on Dixit's results). I now offer this idea to you as a potential key to understanding how we have all become so desensitized to the exchange rate.

I think the best way to convey the point is with a couple of cooked-up numerical examples; we can then turn to the general principle that underlies them.

First, consider a hypothetical Japanese firm that is being battered by the strong yen to the point that at the current exchange rate—say, 120 yen to the dollar—it is losing money on its U.S. sales. This firm is not especially optimistic; it hopes that the yen may return to 140, which would make it profitable again, but regards it as equally likely that the yen will rise to 100, greatly increasing its losses. If that were the whole story, the firm would simply exit immediately. However, the firm has invested heavily in building its U.S. market position, and it knows that if it abandons that position now it will not be worthwhile to try to regain it even if the yen does fall.

Table 2.1 gives some hypothetical numbers for this worried Japanese firm. I suppose that at the current rate of 120 yen per dollar it is losing money at an annual rate of $100 million. If the yen goes back to 140, it will be able to make $100 million annually; if the yen rises to 100, it will lose $300 million per year if it still tries to hang on. Also, I

Table 2.1
Payoffs to a firm delaying exit.

	Yen per dollar	
	100	140
Initial-year loss	−100	−100
PDV[a] of later years	0	900

a. PDV: present discounted value

suppose that the firm discounts future earnings at an annual rate of 10 percent.

The expected returns to this firm from sales in the U.S. market are clearly negative. However, the firm does not have to choose between leaving the U.S. market now and staying forever; its immediate choice is whether to exit now or to wait a year before deciding. Despite current losses, it turns out that the firm should hang in there for one more year.

The table shows the returns to the firm if it chooses to wait a year before making its decision. In the first year the firm loses $100 million. In the second year, it drops out if the yen goes to 100 but stays in if it falls to 140. In this latter case, it will earn $100 million per year thereafter, with a present value discounted to the first year of $900 million. The overall expected present value to the firm of this "wait and see" strategy is therefore the average of what happens if the yen goes to 100 and what happens if it goes to 140: $350 million.

By contrast, if the firm drops out immediately it makes nothing and loses nothing.

In an expected-value sense, the firm is clearly better off holding on and hoping for better times even though it is losing money at the current exchange rate, and *even though it regards an adverse movement in the rate as being as likely as a favorable movement*. Of course, if the firm regarded a return to 140 as more likely than a rise to 100, the case for remaining in the market in the face of losses would be even stronger.

Uncertainty, then, makes firms cautious about exiting from hard-won market positions. It also makes them cautious about investing in acquiring new market positions, as the next example will show.

Consider a U.S. firm, its cost competitiveness restored by the fall in the dollar, that is considering whether to enter an international market in competition with Japan. At the current yen-dollar rate of 120, it knows that it could earn profits large enough to justify the initial cost of entry, and it is reasonably optimistic about the future course of the exchange rate: Like the Japanese firm just described, this American firm regards it as equally likely that the yen will rise to 100 (a rate at which entry would be even more profitable) or fall to 140 (in which case entry would not be profitable).

Some hypothetical numbers for the American firm are given in table 2.2. I suppose that in order to enter it must incur an irreversible cost of $800 million. At the current exchange rate of 120, it can earn an annual surplus of $100 million. If the rate goes to 100, this annual surplus will rise to $200 million; if the rate goes to 140, the surplus will go to

Table 2.2
Entering versus waiting with a favorable exchange rate.

	Yen per dollar	
	100	140
Immediate entry		
First year	−700	−700
PDV in subsequent years	1,800	0
One-year delay		
First year	0	0
PDV in subsequent years	1,080	0

zero. As in the previous example, the discount rate is 10 percent.

The upper half of table 2.2 shows what happens if the firm enters immediately. In the first year the cash flow is of course negative (800 investment less 100 operating surplus); but if the exchange rate is favorable thereafter, the present value of the returns will substantially exceed the cost of setting up. I have chosen the numbers so that the gains in the strong-yen case exceed the losses in the weak-yen case, so that the firm can earn an expected profit of 200 from investing now in competing with Japan. However, it can do even better by waiting a year.

The lower half of the table shows this. By waiting, the firm of course ensures a zero initial-year cash flow. Then, if the yen goes to 140, the firm prudently stays out, entering only if the yen goes to 100. In this case the firm spends its $800 million to enter and receives $200 million per year in subsequent surplus; discounted back to the first year, this is a net present value of 1,080. Thus, the expected present value of the "wait and see" strategy is $540 million—substantially greater than the return from entering immediately.

In each of these examples, uncertainty seems to have created an incentive for firms to remain temporarily in their current position—either in the market or out of it—even though a change in position would be profitable at the current exchange rate, and the firm is assumed to view favorable and unfavorable exchange-rate movements as equally likely. Thus, exchange-rate uncertainty *per se* seems to give rise to trade inertia. But what is the general principle underlying these examples?

The answer suggested by Dixit's work is that the entry and exit decisions of firms engaged in international trade are essentially the purchase and sale of options. A firm that is not now producing for export can be thought of as owning an option to enter in the future; a firm that is currently producing for export in effect owns an option in the possibility of dropping out. The decision to enter or exit involves not only the concrete costs but also the cost of exercising the option of entering or leaving in the future. The implicit cost of exercising these options adds a hidden fixed cost of entry to the visible costs of investment, setting up a distribution network, and so on, and effectively imposes a fixed cost to exit as well. The "range of no change"—the range of exchange rates in which the firm neither enters if it is not in the market nor exits if it is—is therefore widened, perhaps substantially.

Let us push the analogy with financial options a bit further. Consider the case of entry. In deciding to break into the export market, a firm is in effect exercising its option to "buy" an expected future stream of earnings at the expense of a current sunk cost. Now, the owner of an option does not exercise that option as soon as it is in the money (that is, as soon as the market price exceeds the strike price)—if he did, the option would be worthless. The point is that when the market price is only slightly above the strike price, the profitability of exercising the option has much more room to go up than down, making it worthwhile to wait for a better opportunity. Similarly, a firm that considers entering an export market will not want to enter as soon as the expected present value of revenues from selling in that market exceeds the fixed cost of entry; it will prefer to wait and see. (Another way to think about this is the following: If you enter and then the exchange rate moves adversely, you have lost the full decline in the expected value of future earnings. If you fail to enter and the exchange rate moves in a favorable direction, you still have the opportunity to enter later, so you have lost only a fraction of the rise in the expected value of earnings. Thus, in a situation where the exchange rate is just on the margin where entering is profitable, a firm gains by not entering and waiting to see if the exchange rate becomes still more favorable.)

On the down side, the firm will remain in the market for some range of exchange rates in which the exchange rate does not allow it to earn as much as variable costs. Again, remaining in the market carries a value that the firm must sacrifice if it drops out. This value can be interpreted as the shadow price placed on the firm's option to drop out. Like the option of entering, this option will not be exercised as soon as it is "in the money" (i.e., as soon as the firm cannot cover variable costs).

Thus, uncertainty creates an incentive for firms to pursue a "wait and see" attitude, widening the range of no change in which firms neither enter nor exit. And now we come to the important point: The incentive not to act is greater the more volatile the exchange rate. It is a straightforward result from option pricing that the ratio of the market price at which an option is exercised to the strike price is higher the greater is market volatility. Similarly, in the sunk-cost model a firm will wait for a more favorable exchange rate before entering, and will remain in the market for a more unfavorable rate, the greater the perceived future uncertainty of the rate.

I argued above that it is possible for the exchange rate to move so much because it has so little effect. Now I have just argued that the reverse is true: *The exchange rate has so little effect in part because it fluctuates so much.* When the exchange rate is highly volatile, firms are more likely to regard its movements as temporary, so that regressive expectations reduce their response; and even if they do not have regressive expectations, exchange-rate volatility gives them an incentive to adopt a "wait and see" policy that does not respond quickly to exchange-rate changes.

Clearly there is a circularity here, as is illustrated schematically in figure 2.3. I will not go so far as to suppose that the

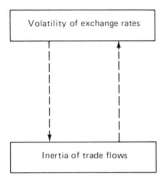

Figure 2.3
A multiplier process on exchange-rate volatility.

process is actually unstable, so that volatility of exchange rates is self-generating. It can be argued, however, that if other factors (such as unstable policy) generate a world of volatile exchange rates, this volatility will grow through a multiplier process: Because exchange rates are volatile, the real economy becomes desensitized to the exchange rate, and because the exchange rate becomes delinked from reality, it becomes free to become even more volatile.

Some Calculations

It is interesting to calculate how wide a range of exchange rates would constitute a "range of no change" using semi-realistic numbers on exchange-rate volatility, real interest rates, and the ratio of sunk to variable costs. Such calculations are, of course, no substitute for real evidence on what firms actually do; but they can at least tell us how important the motivations I have been describing might be in practice.

Table 2.3
Ratio of entry exchange rate to exit exchange rate.

Sunk cost as fraction of variable	Annual variance of real exchange rate		
	0.0	0.0002	0.003
0.0	1.00	1.00	1.00
0.1	1.10	1.18	1.38
0.5	1.50	1.61	1.97

Table 2.3 reports the results of calculating optimal entry and exit strategies for firms whose situation is the following: The logarithm of the exchange rate follows a random walk. The firms must sell at a fixed price in foreign currency if they sell at all; that is, the log of their export price follows the same random walk as the exchange rate. The firms sell a fixed amount (or zero), and they discount future profits at an annual rate of 8 percent.

Now, the calculation of optimal strategies for these hypothetical firms is a good deal more involved than the illustrative examples above might have led you to believe. For one thing, firms do not necessarily decide to enter or exit at the end of a fixed period, as the examples implicitly assumed; instead, firms are always weighing the benefits of acting now against those of waiting and seeing. Also, the decisions to enter and exit are interdependent—when a firm enters, it is in effect purchasing the option to exit at some future date, whereas a firm that exits simultaneously acquires the option to reenter. There is also a nasty little issue involving Jensen's inequality (which receives a full formal treatment in the appendix). A little clever programming allows us to converge on solutions; whether we believe that the result of these calculations is more than a remote metaphor for what firms actually do is an issue to be saved for some other forum.

What table 2.3 shows is the ratio of the exchange rate at which a firm will enter the market to the exchange rate at which it will exit. This ratio is shown as a function of two parameters: the ratio of sunk to variable costs and the annual variance of the exchange rate. For the importance of sunk costs I have no strong priors; a range from zero to half of variable costs seems likely to cover the range of what is reasonable. For the volatility of the exchange rate, three cases are shown. The first is that of zero volatility—that is, what would happen if firms had true static expectations. The second is a variance of 0.0002. This is the actual variance of the real dollar-mark rate over the period 1960–1973 (recall figure 1.4). The last column shows the situation when the variance is 0.003, its actual value for the dollar-mark rate over the period 1973–1986.

It is clear that the increase in volatility under floating rates certainly should have led to greatly increased inertia in entry and exit decisions. If sunk costs are at all important, so that the lower parts of the table are relevant, the shadow fixed costs of entry and exit introduced by volatility may be a large part of the explanation of why highly unstable exchange rates seem to matter so little for the real economy.

Hysteresis

We have now seen that the sunk-cost model can help explain the remarkable lack of response of trade prices and

volumes to large exchange-rate fluctuations and, in particular, why the responsiveness of the real world to the exchange rate seems to have gone down as the variability of
the exchange rate has gone up. However, there is another
important and troubling implication of the sunk cost
model. The model suggests that firms will be reluctant to
respond to the exchange rate in a volatile environment; but
it also suggests that when they finally do react, it will be
difficult to induce them to reverse their decision. Fewer
foreign firms invaded the U.S. market, fewer U.S. firms
abandoned foreign markets, fewer firms with multinational operations shifted their production to weak-
currency countries than one might well have feared given
the huge overvaluation of the dollar in 1984–85; but those
firms that did repond to that overvaluation will not easily
be persuaded to reverse their decisions. In particular, getting the dollar back to where it was in 1980 is not going to
be enough to restore the trade position of 1980.

This is the problem of *hysteresis* in international trade. *Hysteresis* is an ugly but useful word that signifies situations in
which temporary shocks have effects that do not go away
when the shocks are removed. If you push something hard
enough, it will fall over; when you stop pushing, it won't
stand up again. Notice that hysteresis is not the same as
irreversibility: You can pull the unfortunate object back to
an upright position if you want. The point is, however,
that restoring the original environment isn't enough to restore the original results. In recent years economists have
begun to suspect hysteresis in a variety of areas, from technological choice to unemployment rates. The sunk cost
model clearly suggests the possibility of hysteresis in

trade. A level of the dollar that was low enough to deter foreign firms from entering the U.S. market will not necessarily be low enough to induce them to exit once they have incurred the sunk costs needed to break in. A level of the dollar that was low enough to keep U.S. firms competing in foreign markets will not be low enough to persuade them to make the effort to reenter those markets once they have dropped out.

It is important not to misinterpret what hysteresis means for the trade deficit. It does *not* mean that once you have allowed your currency to get severely overvalued you find yourself stuck with a structural trade deficit that never goes away. Budget constraints are still budget constraints, and sooner or later a country must pay its way in the world; hysteresis or no hysteresis, the United States will eventually balance its trade and will indeed run a surplus to service its foreign debt. The question is, instead, at what price this will happen. If the previous strength of the dollar has indeed produced strong hysteretic effects, the United States will not be able to get back on track simply by returning to roughly its previous exchange rate; it will need a period of compensatory undervaluation to regain the markets it has lost. (I am sorry to report, by the way, that the adjectival form of *hysteresis* is, as I have just used it, *hysteretic*, even though I would be happier if it were *hysterical*.)

The Equilibrium Value of the Dollar

Now comes the moment you've all been waiting for—the moment when I tell you what the equilibrium value of the dollar really is, so that you can all run to your brokers.

Over the past few years I have made some exchange-rate forecasts, using a trick I'll describe in lecture 3, that have been more accurate than they deserved to be. So I will now give you a forthright statement about where the dollar must go: *I don't know*.

However, there is one thing I do know: *Secretary Baker doesn't know either*. Neither does Chancellor Lawson, and least of all does Ronald McKinnon. The fact that nobody knows is crucial for the current dilemmas of international monetary policy, with which I will be preoccupied in lecture 3. In the present lecture, let me focus on why the only reasonable position is one of principled agnosticism.

Obviously a major reason for uncertainty is the hysteresis that, I have argued, arises from the combination of sunk costs and volatility in international trade. To the extent that firms made quasi-permanent decisions to enter markets, leave markets, or relocate production when the dollar was strong, we will need a period of dollar weakness to induce them to turn the clock back. This tells us with some certainty that the dollar must fall below its 1980 level, at least for a while; so I can say with considerable assurance that people who look at some kind of purchasing-power-parity index and want to call a halt when the dollar reaches 100 are going to be disappointed—they have taken an indicator and confused it with a theory. This made life easy when the dollar was still noticeably above its 1980 level. But this is no longer true; I would guess fairly strongly that a further fall is still needed, but not as strongly as I did in early 1987.

In principle, of course, the answer is to resolve the issue through hard empirical work, and we should certainly try. However, the stories I have been telling in this lecture suggest that such empirical assessment of the dollar's appropriate level is more difficult than we had previously realized. For one thing, the determination of trade flows as I have sketched it in this lecture is a lot more complicated than the simple income-and-price-elasticity framework that is the workhorse of practical analysis in this field, and which I am as guilty of overusing as anyone else. If the sunk-cost model is at all right, we need fancier modeling and fancier econometrics on trade than anyone has yet done.

Worse yet, the sunk cost model suggests that determination of trade flows and prices is a matter of forward-looking investment decisions—i.e., that it depends on expectations (and also on higher moments of the perceived distributions). This means that trade equations, like many other aspects of macroeconomics, are subject to the Lucas critique. The apparent relationship between the determinants of trade and the outcome will shift when the environment changes. When the environment has been shifting radically and erratically, the past will give us a picture of continuous expectational disequilibrium, as firms attempt to revise their decision rules in the face of an environment they do not fully understand. We should not expect econometric estimates over such a period to yield results that will remain stable, and in fact econometric models of trade that worked well during the first half of the 1980s have fallen apart in the second.

Finally, there is an issue that I have not yet mentioned in this lecture: structural change. Under the dust cloud thrown up by the gyrations of the dollar, there has been a continuing erosion of the United States' once-decisive technological advantage over other advanced countries. In 1970 the United States had higher production costs than Japan (and even Europe) in nearly everything that both the United States and the other nation(s) were able to produce. Yet the United States was able to pay its way in world trade by exporting things that other countries could not (or not yet) produce: newly developed goods, and goods involving highly sophisticated technology. In other words, I am arguing that the sustainable level of the dollar in 1970 partly reflected the rents that the United States was able to appropriate because of its position at the top of the technological ladder. Over the years since 1970, this position has been steadily eroded to the point that it is now questionable that the United States has any lead at all. During the 1970s the eroding United States technological lead was probably the main reason why the real dollar needed to fall an average of about 3 percent a year in real terms. There is no good reason not to suppose that this secular trend continued into the 1980s (how rapid it has been is less clear).

In the end, then, I am quite certain that the dollar needs to be weaker than it was in 1980, and pretty certain that it needs to fall from here (although I don't know how much). The essential problem is that too much water has passed under the bridge since the last time the dollar was at a level that looked sustainable. There is therefore an irreducible and large penumbra of uncertainty around any estimate of the level of the dollar that we now need.

This is a shame, because the behavior of international capital markets in the last decade has created a good case for trying to stabilize exchange rates—*if* we can start from levels that are sustainable for a fairly long run. The collision between the uncertainty I have just described (which militates in favor of a laissez-faire approach to exchange rates) and the misbehavior of international financial markets (which argues for an attempt to impose stability) is the basic dilemma of international monetary policy. That will be the subject of the third lecture.

Appendix: The Dixit Model of Entry and Exit under Exchange-Rate Uncertainty

In lecture 2 I attempted, with the aid of two contrived numerical examples, to present the essential idea that an uncertain exchange rate makes firms reluctant to enter and to exit foreign markets. However, these examples, while they convey the right idea, are not quite right as full descriptions of the options facing firms. In particular, I implicitly assumed two unreasonable things in constructing tables 2.1 and 2.2. The first was that, whereas a firm had the option of delaying its decision to enter or exit this year, one year from now it was compelled to decide—it could not wait still another year. Second, the tables implicitly assume that the decision to enter or leave is final—that there is no possibility of reentering or dropping out at some later date. Clearly, neither of these assumptions is right. A firm does not face an arbitrary cutoff date by which it must enter or exit; instead, it must at each point in time weigh the benefits of moving now against the additional benefits of waiting. Furthermore, if a firm exits, part of the value of its new position is the possibility of reentering under more favorable conditions; if it enters, the value of that move is enhanced by the possibility of leaving again later.

To do the analysis properly, we need a full treatment of the problem. Such a treatment has recently been developed by Avinash Dixit (1987a). In this appendix I present my own version of Dixit's model. The results are, I believe, useful and interesting—in particular, they underlie the results reported in table 2.3.

Consider a firm that is able to sell a good in a foreign market. For simplicity, assume that the price level in each country is stable in domestic currency. Assume also that if the firm does decide to produce, it must first incur a fixed cost F in domestic currency, and that it thereafter receives a constant stream of revenues in *foreign* currency. What it cares about, however, is its revenues in domestic currency. Let P denote the value of the revenue per period in domestic currency; P will be a random variable, moving with the exchange rate.

The fixed cost F is also, by assumption, a sunk cost; that is, if the firm exits it cannot recover F, and if it chooses to reenter it must incur the fixed cost all over again. The firm also must incur variable costs in order to produce for the foreign market. We will choose units so that these variable costs are equal to unity in domestic currency. Thus, at any point in time, the firm, if it is producing for export, earns an operating surplus at the rate $P - 1$.

As it turns out, it will be useful to work with the logarithm of the revenues received from exports. We will denote this as p. The operating surplus is then $e^p - 1$.

Clearly the decision to enter or to exit is in some sense an investment decision, requiring that the firm discount future profits at some rate. Assume that the firm is risk-neutral, with a constant discount rate r.

Finally, we must make some assumption about the distribution of the exchange rate. Following Dixit, let us assume that the exchange rate follows a logarithmic random walk—or, rather, since we will want to work in continuous time, a diffusion process of the form

$$dp = \sigma dz, \tag{A.1}$$

which implies a variance over a time interval t of $\sigma^2 t$.

The economics of an assumption like A.1 are problematic. There is no good reason why the real exchange rate should follow a random walk; indeed, unless technological shocks follow an unlikely pattern, it by and large cannot do so. In reality there is no question that real exchange rates exhibit a tendency to revert to equilibrium values, although this mean reversion is difficult to pick up statistically owing to the combination of high volatility and structural change, which alters equilibrium rates over time. The utility of assuming exchange-rate behavior without mean reversion is twofold. First, it helps us isolate the "option" aspect of unresponsiveness to exchange rates. As I pointed out in the lecture, it is easy to see why firms will not respond to an exchange-rate change if they think it is temporary; a more surprising insight is that they may not respond even if they regard it as equally likely to go either way. Second, since actual exchange-rate data *look* a lot like a random walk (although I am sure that they are not), this diffusion process makes it straightforward to map from actual exchange-rate behavior into a parameter of our model.

We have now defined a minimal model of the factors determining the entry and exit decisions of a firm under uncertain exchange rates. Let us now consider how to define the firm's maximization problem.

The Firm's Maximization Problem

In this simple model, the firm has only one choice at each moment. If it is in the market, it can choose to leave; if it is out, it can choose to enter. In order to make this choice, it must assign a *value* to the state of being either in or out of the market. These values of course depend on the exchange rate, or (what is the same thing) on the current value of p. Thus, there is a value function, $V_I(p)$, that defines how much it is worth to be in the market, and another value function, $V_O(p)$, that defines how much it is worth to be out.

As a first step toward defining these value functions, note that the expected rate of change of the value need not be zero even though the exchange rate follows a random walk. Following the usual rules of stochastic calculus, when p follows equation A.1 the expected rates of change of the values of being in or out depend on the second derivative and on volatility:

$$E[dV_I(p)/dt] = (\sigma^2/2)V_I''(p), \tag{A.2}$$

$$E[dV_O(p)/dt] = (\sigma^2/2)V_O''(p). \tag{A.3}$$

Let us now determine the forms of the two value functions, beginning with $V_I(p)$. The easiest way to proceed is to recognize that the value of being in the market is in effect a kind of asset, which must offer the same return as alternative assets. The return on being in the market consists of two elements: the operating surplus earned by the firm, and the expected capital gain or loss on the value of being in the market itself. These two returns together must yield a rate of return r. Thus, we have

$$e^p - 1 + E[dV_I(p)/dt] = rV_I(p) \tag{A.4}$$

or, using equation A.2,

$$V_I(p) = e^p/r - 1/r + (1/r)E[dV_I(p)/dt]$$

$$= e^p/r - 1/r + (\sigma^2/2r)V_I''(p). \tag{A.5}$$

Next we make a guess at the form of $V_I(p)$. Through trial and error, we discover that the following form works:

$$V_I(p) = Me^p - 1/r + Ae^{pp} + Be^{-pp}, \tag{A.6}$$

where M, ρ, A, and B all need to be determined.

We know from equation A.6 that

$$V_I''(p) = Me^p + \rho^2(Ae^{pp} + Be^{-pp}). \tag{A.7}$$

Next we substitute back into equation A.5:

$$Me^p - 1/r + Ae^{\rho p} + Be^{-\rho p} = e^p/r - 1/r + (\sigma^2/2r)Me^p$$
$$+ (\sigma^2\rho^2/2r)(Ae^{\rho p} + Be^{-\rho p}).$$

$$(A.8)$$

Now, equation A.8 must hold for all values of p; this enables us to pin down the values of M and ρ immediately. Grouping all terms containing e^p, we get

$$M[1 - (\sigma^2/2r)]e^p = e^p/r,$$

which implies that

$$M = 1/(r - \sigma^2/2). \qquad (A.9)$$

Similarly, grouping together all terms containing $Ae^{\rho p} + Be^{-\rho p}$, we have

$$Ae^{\rho p} + Be^{-\rho p} = (\sigma^2\rho^2/2r)(Ae^{\rho p} + Be^{-\rho p}),$$

which implies

$$\rho = (2r/\sigma^2)^{1/2}. \qquad (A.10)$$

This implies the following general form for the function $V_I(p)$:

$$[1/(r - \sigma^2/2)]e^p - 1/r + Ae^{\rho p} + Be^{-\rho p}.$$

Of the four terms in this function, the first two together represent the capitalized value of expected operating surplus. Notice that this is not quite equal to $(P - 1)/r$, as one might expect from the fact that p follows a random walk. The reason is Jensen's inequality: It is the logarithm of P, not P itself, that follows a random walk, and the expectation of a log is not the log of an expectation. Aside from this correction, the first two terms in effect represent the valuation of the firm under static expectations.

The other two terms represent a deviation from this valuation, and we can use this interpretation to further simplify the expression. If we assume that the deviation of valuation from its "fundamental" level must be bounded in absolute value, then, since p can rise without limit, we must have $A = 0$. We do not have a corresponding restriction on B, since at some sufficiently low p the firm will drop out of the market. Thus, the final form of the value function is

$$V_I(p) = [1/(r - \sigma^2/2)]e^p + Be^{-\rho p}. \tag{A.11}$$

Next we turn to the value of being out of the market. In this case there is, of course, no operating surplus, so the rate-of-return equation is simply

$$E[dV_O(p)/dt] = r\,V_O(p). \tag{A.12}$$

Using equation A.3, this becomes

$$(\sigma^2/2)V_O''(p) = r\,V_O(p), \tag{A.13}$$

or

$$V_O(p) = (\sigma^2/2r)V_O''(p). \tag{A.14}$$

We make a guess at the functional form of $V_O(p)$:

$$V_O(p) = Ce^{\rho p} + De^{-\rho p}, \tag{A.15}$$

which implies

$$V_O''(p) = \rho^2(Ce^{\rho p} + De^{-\rho p}) \tag{A.16}$$

and thus, substituting into equation A.14, that

$$\rho = (2r/\sigma^2)^{1/2}. \tag{A.17}$$

We can also invoke a boundary condition similar to that we used for V_I to simplify the function. Being out of the market carries value only because of the possibility of profitably entering at some future date. At arbitrarily low values of p, this possibility should become sufficiently remote that the value of the option of entry becomes zero, which can be true only if $D = 0$. So the final form of the value function is

$$V_O(p) = Ce^{\rho p}. \tag{A.18}$$

We have now determined the value functions of being in and out of the market up to one parameter in each case: B in equation A.11 and C in equation A.18. In economic terms, these represent the deviations from "fundamental" values introduced by the possibility of exiting while in and the possibility of entering when out. To determine these remaining parameters, then, we need to examine optimal entry and exit.

Optimal Entry and Exit

A firm will enter whenever it can raise its value by more than the fixed cost of entry, and will exit whenever it is worth more out of the market than in. Since the valuations depend only on the current p, this clearly means that there must be some price (p^I) at which a firm that is out will come in and some price (p^O) at which a firm that is in will drop out. It must be true that

$$V_I(p^I) = V_O(p^I) + F \tag{A.19}$$

and also that

$$V_I(p^O) = V_O(p^O). \tag{A.20}$$

However, these conditions by themselves do not suffice to determine p^I and p^O, since the value functions themselves still have one free parameter each. To tie down the model, we need two more conditions: the "smooth pasting" conditions

$$V_I'(p^I) = V_O'(p^I) \tag{A.21}$$

and

$$V'_I(p^O) = V'_O(p^O). \tag{A.22}$$

The "smooth pasting" condition is not yet a completely familiar part of the international economist's toolbox— Dixit's papers were my own first introduction to it—and may thus be worth an attempt at intuitive explanation.

To get some intuition, let us briefly imagine, instead of a continuous-time stochastic process, a random walk in which p moves up or down by an amount δ each period with equal probability. (By making the time period shorter, we can use such a discrete random walk to approximate the diffusion process as closely as we like.)

In this discrete-time setting, p^O would be the highest level of p at which the value of a firm that drops out exceeds that of one that remains in unless the price drops still lower. In particular, it must be more profitable to drop out at p^O than to wait until the price drops to $p^O - \delta$.

Figure A.1 shows a magnified view of $V_I(p)$ and $V_O(p)$ in the neighborhood of p^O. Of course, the two functions in-

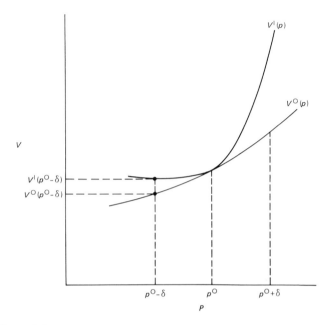

Figure A.1
Why the value functions are tangent.

tersect at p^O, and at higher p than this $V_I(p)$ exceeds $V_O(p)$. However, the picture is also drawn with V_I above V_O at *lower p*—and, in particular, $V_I(p^O - \delta) > V_O(p^O - \delta)$.

To see why this must be the correct drawing, we need to apply a sort of backwards logic. We know that p^O can be the right price at which to drop out only if at the price the firm is more valuable out of the market than in. By the way we have constructed $V_I(p)$, the value we show as $V_I(p^O)$ is the value that the firm will place on being in the market if there is an equal probability next period that the value will be $V_I(p^O - \delta)$ and $V_I(p^O + \delta)$. Suppose that the firm were *not* to drop out at p^O but were instead to drop out at $p^O - \delta$. Then if the price were to fall next period, the firm would be worth $V_O(p^O - \delta) < V_I(p^O - \delta)$—implying that this period's value would be less than $V_I(p^O)$. This shows that the firm does in fact do better by dropping out now rather than waiting for a still lower p.

On the other hand, suppose that we had drawn the figure with $V_I(p^O - \delta)$ *below* $V_O(p^O - \delta)$. Then the value attached to a strategy of dropping out at $p^O - \delta$ rather than p^O would exceed $V_I(p^O)$—showing that this was not the right choice of p^O!

Thus, if p^O is chosen correctly, it must be true not only that $V_I(p^O)$ equals $V_O(p^O)$ but also that *both* $V_I(p^O + \delta)$ and $V_I(p^O - \delta)$ lie above $V_O(p)$. As we make the time period, and hence δ, arbitrarily short, this leads to the conclusion that $V_I(p)$ must be *tangent* to $V_O(p)$ at p^O—which is the "smooth pasting" condition.

A similar logic applies at p^I, except that there $V_O(p)$ must be just tangent to $V_I(p) - F$, lying below it at both higher and lower prices.

Figure A.2 shows the actual value functions calculated for $F = 0.8$, $r = 0.08$, and $\sigma^2 = 0.03$.

To calculate these value functions, we need to simultaneously solve for four variables: the free parameters in each of the value functions, and the entry and exit prices. The four equations are the entry and exit conditions

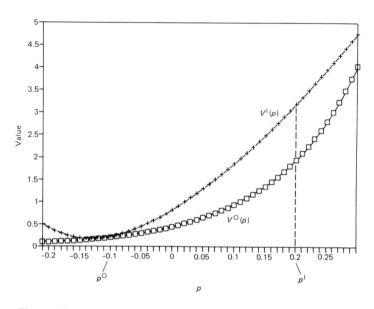

Figure A.2
Value functions for Dixit's model.

$V_I(p^I) = V_O(p^I) + F,$

$V_I(p^O) = V_O(p^O)$

and the "smooth pasting" conditions

$V_I'(p^I) = V_O'(p^I),$

$V_I'(p^O) = V_O'(p^O).$

Writing these out explicitly, we have

$$[1/(r - \sigma^2/2)]e^{p^O} - 1/r + Be^{-\rho p^O} = Ce^{\rho p^O}, \tag{A.23}$$

$$[1/(r - \sigma^2/2)]e^{p^O} - \rho B^{-\rho p^O} = \rho Ce^{\rho p^O}, \tag{A.24}$$

$$[1/(r - \sigma^2/2)]e^{p^I} - 1/r + Be^{-\rho p^I} = Ce^{\rho p^O} + F, \tag{A.25}$$

$$[1/(r - \sigma^2/2)]e^{p^I} - \rho B^{-\rho p^I} = \rho C e^{\rho p^I}. \tag{A.26}$$

These equations may then be solved for B, C, p^I, and p^O. (A helpful hint for those trying to do this numerically: It is a good idea to make a guess at C, solve for B and p^O given this guess, then solve for C and p_I given this estimate of B and alternate until convergence.)

3

Financial Markets and the International Monetary System

In lecture 2 I argued that an important part of the explanation of the instability of exchange rates in the 1980s is a multiplier process: Unstable exchange rates make firms cautious, unwilling to change their production and pricing decisions in response to the exchange rate; the delinking of exchange rates from reality then allows the exchange rates to become still more unstable; and so on. This explanation tells us why an initial source of instability can have a magnified effect, but not where the origins of the instability lie. In this final lecture I will discuss the origins of exchange-rate instability and then move to a consideration of the problems of exchange-rate policy.

Of course, a major source of exchange-rate instability lies in well-understood instabilities of economic policy and other underlying forces. The remarkable combination of U.S. fiscal irresponsibility with disinflationary monetary policy had a lot to do with the rise of the dollar in the first half of the 1980s; fluctuations in the price of oil have played their role in the exchange rates of both energy-rich countries (such as the United Kingdom) and energy-poor countries (e.g. Japan). However, I am going to argue that this is not the whole story. Exchange-rate instability has resulted not only from reasonable market responses to changes in policies and underlying conditions but also from failures in the international financial markets. In particular, the traditional fear that floating exchange rates will be subject to destabilizing speculation—to speculative bubbles that do real harm—is, unfortunately, strongly supported by the evidence of the 1980s.

This is a highly controversial (although of course correct) position. In questioning the reliability of international financial markets I am challenging both the cherished views of economists and the preconceptions of most lay observers. It is one thing to question the functioning of global markets for goods and services, which are not very different in appearance today from what they were in the past; however, most people imagine that—at least in the case of financial markets—borders either have disappeared or are about to. After all, computers and satellite transmission have created financial markets that almost never sleep and that can transfer billions of dollars across the world in seconds. Surely whatever imperfectness there is in the linkages between countries lies in the dull traditional world of freighters and longshoremen, not in the glittering modern world of international finance.

Alas, appearances can be deceiving—especially when you are dealing with financiers, who thrive on appearance. It is a mistake to emphasize the technology of international capital transfer instead of the effectiveness with which that technology is used—a mistake of confusing inputs with outputs. We do indeed have wonderful technology of information processing and information transfer, but the awesome technical prowess of the modern financial world has simply further reduced transaction costs that were already too small to matter very much at a macroeconomic level. Meanwhile, the use to which the technology is put is, in the light of what is possible in principle and what has actually happened in the past, disappointing. Our great-grandfathers, armed with ledger books and telegraphs, created a far more extensive capital market than we have managed to create with our computers and satellites. Further, while the modern capital markets can process orders of magnitude more information than those of the past, their success at *using* information—that is, at making sensible judgments based on the facts at hand—has been worse in the 1980s than anyone might have expected.

I will devote the first part of this lecture to explaining the extent to which international financial markets have fallen short of the performance that we might have expected on the bases of logic and experience, and will conclude with a discussion of the problematic implications of that poor performance for exchange-rate policy.

The Performance of International Financial Markets

The Integration of Capital Markets

In 1980 Martin Feldstein and Charles Horioka published a paper that has been at the center of great controversy. They questioned the common assumption that modern capital markets are highly integrated, arguing that the evidence suggested rather limited integration. The way they presented their results has given rise to a lot of confusion, most of it not their fault. Let me try to put their result a different way, and explain why I believe that they were right in pointing out the existence of a puzzle.

The basic observation of Feldstein and Horioka is the following: There is very little transfer of capital from high-saving to low-saving countries. Within the OECD, savings rates during the period 1960–1985 ranged from 8 percent (in the United States) to 21 percent (in Japan). If savings were transferred by a well-integrated international capital market, we should expect to see a comparably wide range of current-account balances. Yet in fact, current accounts have fluctuated within much narrower bands, and if we look at long averages of such balances—averaging out the occasional spikes—the range of sustained transfers of resources has been really narrow. I illustrate the point with a scatter plot in figure 3.1. If we had a fully integrated capital market, with an exogenous distribution of savings rates, these points should lie on the 45° line. The reality is that they are instead closely clustered around the x axis. (The clustering would be even stronger if we ignored the lower left point, which is the Republic of Ireland.)

I have deliberately stated the point here in a different way from Feldstein and Horioka, and plotted the results differently, because doing it this way makes it clearer that the main challenges that have been offered to the result are unconvincing. In the original paper, the statement was

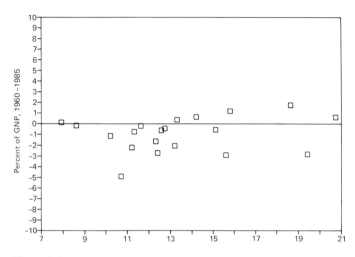

Figure 3.1
Savings rates versus current accounts.

couched in terms of the relationship between savings and investment rates (which is of course just the same thing, since the investment rate is by definition equal to the savings rate minus the current account). The attempts to explain away the result have focused on reasons why investment and saving might be correlated; the implausibility of these explanations is more apparent when the data are presented as they are here. A variety of considerations might lead to a correlation of national savings and investment rates even in a world of perfect capital mobility—for example, high rates of population or total factor productivity growth might raise both the savings rate and the demand for investment. However, it is hard to explain why this should match up savings and investment so perfectly that there are only minor net capital flows.

The scale of capital flows is also remarkably small in the light of experience. In the late nineteenth century and the early twentieth, massive capital flows were taken for granted. Great Britain ran a current-account surplus over the period 1870–1914 that *averaged* more than 5 percent of GNP. During the period 1900–1913 Canada's average current deficit was more than 5 percent of GNP, and the figure for 1910–1913 was 13 percent. In a world of high capital mobility, such large capital flows are what we would expect—while savings rates and investment rates may be correlated, we would also expect to find substantial differences between the world distribution of savings and the world distribution of investment opportunities.

Why are capital flows so much smaller in the 1980s than they were before 1914? I am not sure, but I would guess that a major reason is the increase in actual interference and the even greater increase in potential interference by the state. Some major industrial countries (including Japan, France, and Italy) maintained effective capital controls during the 1970s. Further, even those countries that currently maintain open capital markets cannot be relied on to do so in all circumstances—not even the United States. For example, if foreign ownership of U.S. businesses, or the burden of foreign debt service on the U.S. balance of payments, or the effects of foreign capital flight on the U.S. dollar become a political issue at some future point, might not the United States restrict the mobility or the rights of foreign capital in a way that would reduce its value? In the welfare-state capitalism of the modern world, it is not possible to have the simple confidence that property rights will be respected that many international investors had in the golden age of capital mobility.

Now, the 1980s have been marked by the removal of the most visible capital restrictions in the industrial world. Japanese investors have been given access to overseas assets, and France and Italy are dismantling their capital restraints as part of the process of financial integration within Europe. Furthermore, the experience of the 1980s has seemed to suggest that capital is more mobile than the earlier evidence indicated. After all, when the U.S. budget deficit rose in the 1980s, the current-account deficit rose by an almost exactly equal amount. To put it another way, all the crowding out took place in the trade balance, none of it in domestic investment. This is just what one would have expected if the United States were a small open economy facing perfect capital mobility; therefore, it is a piece of evidence that reinforces the case that capital is actually quite mobile.

There are some problems with this case. For one thing, the results were actually too good to be true—even if the United States is open to perfect capital mobility, it is *not* a small open economy, and therefore some domestic crowding out should have occurred. This crowding out should have been reinforced by the perceived temporariness of the dollar appreciation that accompanied capital inflow: Investors should have required a real interest differential in order to hold dollars, and this should have concentrated crowding out disproportionately on the United States. A back-of-the-envelope calculation suggests that, even with perfect capital mobility, only half of the budget deficit—not all of it—should have spilled over into the current account.

I would guess that several factors explain why capital appeared to be so mobile. First, the U.S. budget deficit was only one of several factors pushing toward a reallocation of savings flows toward the United States; fiscal contraction in Europe and Japan and the increased investment demand resulting from accelerated depreciation in the United States also worked in the same direction. A liberalization of restrictions on capital outflow in Japan also helped release a huge pool of savings to the world market. Finally, errors of judgment by investors also contributed to the size of the capital inflow. Investors did not realize how large a trade deficit, and therefore how large a capital inflow, would result from the levels to which they pushed the dollar; they also continued to buy dollars without, apparently, realizing the extent to which they necessarily faced capital losses as the dollar declined.

In retrospect, the remarkable extent to which the United States was able to finance its savings decline by borrowing abroad may turn out to have been a fluke. The next surge in demand for funds by an industrial country will probably not be matched by a comparable set of favorable circumstances. Despite the apparent evidence in favor of capital-market integration offered by recent U.S. experience, I remain a skeptic about how much integration we have really achieved.

However, the key questions about international capital markets are not how much capital flows but whether it flows at the right time and in the right direction. That is, however integrated the capital markets may be, we should be even more concerned with how *sensible* they are. And it is here that the 1980s have not been encouraging at all.

Speculative Efficiency

I have raised some doubts about whether international financial markets are really as effective at transferring resources as they are supposed to be. This is important; however, for exchange-rate policy, which is the main theme of these lectures, another aspect of the functioning of financial markets is more important: Can the markets be trusted? That is, will the markets, left to themselves, work in a sensible way, or are they characterized by speculative bubbles, systematic short-sightedness, or others of the sins of which they are sometimes accused? The question of the trustworthiness of exchange markets has always been at the center of debates over the appropriate exchange-rate regime. In the 1940s Ragnar Nurkse's classic study of international currency experience found exchange markets guilty of speculative runs, irrational behavior, and disruptive effects on world stability—a view that helped form the consensus in favor of a tightly managed system such as Bretton Woods. In his classic defense of floating rates, Milton Friedman argued that exchange markets would never be subject to destabilizing speculation *per se*, because this would be unprofitable for investors—that is, that we could rely on the self-interest of the speculators to keep the markets sensible. At the present time, although there may be academic arguments that a target-zone regime would help promote policy coordination, it is surely the volatility of the markets rather than such abstract considerations that induces the G7 monetary authorities to keep on trying to stabilize rates.

In the academic environment of the 1980s, the natural and automatic response of most trained economists is that Friedman must have been right. The efficient-markets hypothesis has so dominated thinking about financial markets that few remember that it is a hypothesis rather than a fact. And it is not widely admitted in international economics, or appreciated outside it, that the evidence is in fact pretty close to decisive against the efficient-markets hypothesis for foreign exchange markets.

The simplest efficient-market model, and the one that most informs the current thinking, is that of a market in which risk premia are small and may be neglected. If risk premia are zero, then the forward rate should be an efficient predictor, and certainly an unbiased predictor, of the future spot rate. Equivalently, the interest differential, which must equal the forward premium up to (tiny) transaction costs, should be an unbiased predictor of the subsequent change in the spot rate.

Of course this model neglects risk premia; but whenever data seem to indicate that forward rates *are* unbiased predictors, this is claimed as evidence in favor of the efficient-markets hypothesis. Thus, during the early years of floating exchange rates, investigators looked at data from

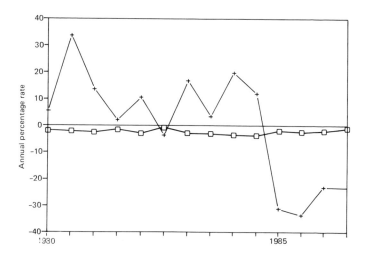

Figure 3.2
Expectations and the dollar-mark rate. □ : interest difference;
+ : actual change.

the 1920s, found what they thought was evidence of un-
biasedness (mostly incorrectly, but that is not my current
concern), and used this evidence to defend the case for
speculative efficiency in forward exchange as a general
proposition. Thus, it is interesting to ask what the evidence from the 1980s looks like.

Figure 3.2 is a plot of two series: the difference between
German and U.S. interest rates, and the actual rate of
change in the dollar-mark rate over the subsequent half-
year. It is immediately apparent that the interest differential has been a poor predictor of the subsequent actual
change, but that is not the important point. More important is the fact that there have been predictable elements in
the exchange rate that the interest differential has not

pointed to, and that, to the extent that the interest differential did change, it more often than not pointed the wrong way. The movements in the dollar have shown substantial serial correlation (figure 3.2 shows half-yearly changes, of which nine out of ten were positive in the period 1980–1985) while the interest differential has been small and stable; when the interest differential did change, it seemed to be in the wrong way (e.g., the interest differential has been smaller since the dollar began declining than when it was rising). Formal tests confirm this picture: Regressions of changes in the spot rate on forward premia have a negative coefficient, and the forward market's prediction errors are serially correlated.

At the very least, we have to say that the evidence offers no positive support for the view that the foreign-exchange market is an efficient information processor. However, two defenses may be offered for the market's rationality. The first is that there may have been large and shifting risk premia. The second is the "peso problem": Large potential events that did not happen to occur within the sample may have been influencing expectations.

It is hard to refute definitively an explanation that is based on risk premia, since such premia in effect give defenders of the market a dummy variable with which to explain each observation. However, several considerations make it doubtful that risk plays a large role in explaining the failure of interest differentials to provide unbiased predictions. For one thing, it is hard to believe that the risk premia are that large and that volatile. Over the period 1980–1985, the dollar's appreciation plus the dollar-mark interest differential provided a rate-of-return differential of no less than 13.7 percent. Since the dollar's rise was highly serially correlated, most of this rise would have been predicted, so the risk premium would have to have been enormous. Meanwhile, *a priori* estimates of risk premia for foreign exchange based on historical volatility and plausible risk aversion suggest that they should be very small. Furthermore, we have again seen serially correlated movements in the exchange rate as the dollar has declined; if this is to be explained by risk premia, we need a massive shift in the premium from positive to negative as well.

The implied historical pattern of prediction errors also makes a risk-premium explanation implausible. From 1980 to 1985 the interest differential consistently underpredicted the dollar's rise (actually, it pointed the wrong way); then the differential consistently underpredicted its fall. To explain this experience in terms of risk premia, one must argue that the dollar was perceived as highly risky when it was rising and the mark as highly risky when the dollar was falling. That is, one would need to believe that the dollar rose despite an increased perception that it was a risky investment, and that it fell despite a revised perception that it had become a good investment—the opposite of what "safe haven" explanations of the dollar's rise and fall would tell us.

Not incidentally, the direct evidence on expectations, from the survey data collected and analyzed by Jeffrey Frankel and Kenneth Froot, does not support the idea that the combination of an interest differential in favor of the United States and a persistently rising dollar can be attributed to risk. Indeed, the survey data suggest that participants in the market expected the dollar to fall even *more* rapidly than the interest differential.

The "peso problem" is now a familiar way of explaining how a market may seem to make persistent errors. Suppose that there is a large event (the usual examples are a hyperinflation if you don't already have one in progress, or a monetary stabilization if you do) to which people rationally assign some low probability but which turns out not to occur. Then this potential event, by its very size, will influence behavior in ways that a future historian, knowing that the event did not happen, might regard as evidence of market inefficiency. Money spent on earthquake insurance in California is, on the econometric evidence, a persistently low-return investment. Similarly, a potential devaluation may give rise to a persistent interest differential that looks inefficient if the currency never actually gets devalued.

The "peso problem" explanation for serially correlated deviations between the interest differential and the subsequent change in the dollar is that when the dollar was rising people consistently assigned some weight to the possibility of a sudden collapse, and that when it was falling they correspondingly assigned some weight to the possibility of a sudden rise.

It is difficult to refute the peso problem as an explanation of any apparently inefficient behavior, since it rests on what didn't happen rather than what did. However, there are some ways around this. Suppose we can define the large event that the market considers possible; then we can infer from the observed bias in expectations the probability that the market would have to have attached to that event in order to make the *ex ante* bias zero. If the required probability is so high that the event should have been observed in the sample, then we may reject the peso problem as an explanation of the bias. From the first half of 1980 to the first half of 1985 the average annual rate of dollar appreciation against the mark exceeded the interest differential by 13.7 percent. Suppose that the peso problem was caused by a fear that the dollar would suddenly fall back to its 1980 level. On average over this period, the dollar exceeded its 1980 level against the mark by 33 percent. Thus, to explain the bias we need an expectation that the dollar would collapse with an annual probability of $13.7/33 = 0.415$. Since the dollar went five years without collapsing, the probability of this happening was, under the peso-problem hypothesis, only $0.585^5 = 0.068$. If the peso problem explains the events, then, the world we actually turned out to live in was an unlikely draw. By the usual rules of statistical inference, we can turn this around and question the validity of the peso-problem hypothesis.

For the period when the dollar was on its way down, the peso-problem explanation is even harder to justify, since the market would have had to believe that there was some possibility of a sudden rise in the dollar. Yet the dollar clearly needed to fall—something that the market seems to have failed to recognize. Indeed, it is quite clear that the dollar at its peak was riding on a speculative bubble that anyone with a little common sense and readily available data should have been able to diagnose (that, of course, means me). The fact that the dollar went so high, in a way that made no sense even at the time, is another dismaying piece of evidence that foreign-exchange markets are not to be trusted.

Speculative Bubbles

In early 1985 the dollar was, as anyone who was willing to look could see, at an unreasonable level. Although the differential in interest rates between the United States and other industrial countries justified an exchange rate above the dollar's long-run sustainable level, the actual level was much higher than could be justified. I and a few others argued then that the strength of the dollar represented a huge market error. What is important now is not that events have made that analysis look better than it deserves, but the simplicity of the argument and the implications of the fact that exchange markets could go so far astray.

The key point is that the willingness of investors to hold dollar-denominated assets, given the interest differential between these assets and assets denominated in other currencies, amounts to an implicit forecast of the future path of the dollar. If dollar assets pay only 3 percent more than mark assets, then the market is implicitly betting that the dollar will not, on average, decline more than 3 percent per year against the mark. At any point in time we can make our own judgment of whether this forecast is reasonable. When the dollar was at its peak, it was clear from even crude calculations that the market's forecast was not reasonable, because it implied an explosive path for U.S. external debt.

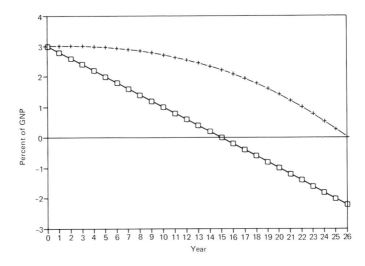

Figure 3.3
Hypothetical path for balances for payments. □ : trade deficit;
+ : current deficit.

The argument runs as follows: In early 1985, nobody thought that the dollar could remain at its then-current level forever. However, the willingness of investors to keep buying dollar assets with only a modest interest incentive implied that they believed that the dollar's decline would be gradual. As the dollar declined, the U.S. *trade deficit* could be expected to decline as well (never mind the problems we have been having since 1985). However, the *current-account deficit* would decline more slowly, because as long as that account is in deficit there will be a growing burden of interest payments on external debt. So the picture of the U.S. balance of payments that had to be implicit in the beliefs of the market in 1985 looked like figure 3.3: a slow decline in the trade deficit, and an even slower decline in the current-account deficit, with the latter going into surplus only when the dollar had declined enough to produce a trade surplus equal to net interest payments.

The question that nobody seems to have asked is how much debt would be accumulated along the way. Notice that what is illustrated in figure 3.3 is actually a sort of race between improving trade balances and rising interest payments; if the trade balance declines slowly, a lot of debt may be accumulated before the debt stops rising.

Indeed, if the trade balance declines too slowly, the implicit forecast of the market might imply an explosive path for debt, as is illustrated in figure 3.4. Here the growth in

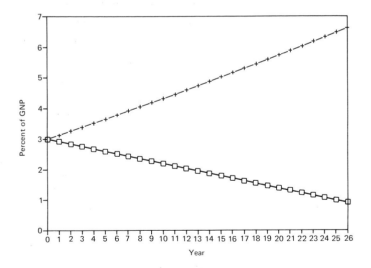

Figure 3.4
Hypothetical path for balances of payments. □ : trade deficit;
+ : current deficit.

interest payments outpaces the decline in the trade deficit, so the debt grows at an accelerating pace. Now, this cannot happen; if tracing out the consequences of the market's implicit forecast says that it will, then that forecast is wrong. In particular, it shows that *the dollar must decline more rapidly than the market now expects*—meaning that part of the dollar's strength represents a speculative bubble. When the market realizes that the dollar must fall more rapidly than it previously expected, the result is the bursting of that bubble.

You already know the punchline: At its peak, a huge deviation of the dollar from its current-balance level was supported by only a modest real interest differential, so that even the roughest estimates implied either runaway debt accumulation or a debt accumulation so large that the United States would become a giant Brazil. It was easy to see that the market was making a mistake, and with 20-20 hindsight the extent of that mistake is breathtaking. The end result of the expectational failure of the foreign-exchange markets has been a huge, largely unrecognized misallocation of investment resources. Suppose, for example, that over the period 1982–1986 Japan's current-account surpluses had been invested in yen, at the prevailing interest rates, rather then in dollars. Then, at a rate of 140 yen to the dollar, the cumulative value of the investment would have exceeded its actual value by $84 billion. This $84 billion did not represent a transfer to the United States; it represented a pure deadweight loss from putting resources in the wrong place.

A Verdict on the Foreign-Exchange Market

On the evidence of the 1980s, the foreign-exchange market seems to make two kinds of errors: It fails to recognize short-run trends, so that forecast errors are serially correlated, and it loses sight of long-run equilibrium, so that it runs away in temporary speculative bubbles.

This may seem like a lot of generalization from the evidence, and it is. However, the pattern I have described is similar to what one finds for the stock market. James Poterba and Lawrence Summers have found that stock prices exhibit serially correlated excess returns in the short run and mean reversion in the long run; these findings correspond nicely to the serially correlated forecast errors and the unperceived tendency to return to long-run equilibrium that I claim to find in exchange rates. In fact, the negative evidence on efficiency in exchange markets is part of a growing body of observations that has undermined the comfortable view that the evidence supports market efficiency. It doesn't—not in a positive sense, anyway. It is still possible to offer sophisticated arguments that save the efficient-markets hypothesis from the data, but these are looking more and more like Ptolemaic epicycles. If you are not deeply committed to the view that financial markets must be efficient, then you will not be comforted by the evidence.

But what difference does it make? The answer goes back to my characterization of the classic positions in the debate over the appropriate exchange regime. The traditional argument against floating rates has been that financial markets cannot be trusted with the determination of something as important as the exchange rate. If the markets looked steady and reliable, this argument could be dismissed. Unfortunately, they do not.

Up to this point I have *described* the world in various ways. The point, however, is to *change* it. What does the analysis I have presented say about exchange-rate policy?

Exchange-Rate Policy

The canonical policy question in international monetary economics is that of the right exchange-rate regime: fixed, floating, or somewhere in between. Contrary to what is usual for economists, this is not a question that breaks down along left/right, perfect-market/imperfect-market, or salt-water/fresh-water (New England/Midwest) lines. Advocates of flexible rates may be Keynesians who want to change relative prices without changing nominal wages, or monetarists who want to keep national control over the monetary aggregates. Advocates of fixed rates may be new

Table 3.1
Canonical positions on the exchange regime.

	For fixed rates	For floating rates
"Fresh-water"	Need for world monetary anchor	Freedom to target aggregates
"Salt-water"	Instability of financial markets	Need to change relative prices

classical economists who believe that prices are perfectly flexible and want a new monetary anchor, or interventionists who fear destabilizing speculation.

Let me recapitulate what I hope I have conveyed in these lectures. In the first lecture I argued that real exchange rates have to be changed as part of the process of adjusting the balance of payments, and that because of the stickiness of prices this is an argument for adjusting the nominal exchange rate in response to disequilibrium. This is the standard Keynesian case for flexible exchange rates, modernized a bit.

In the second lecture I introduced a qualification to that happy picture. I showed what everyone now suspects: that there is some slippage in the gears of the mechanism by which payments are adjusted. More important, I argued that this delinking of exchange rates and reality may be due in large part to the volatility of exchange rates, and that this may be a mutually reinforcing process—that the real world becomes desensitized to unstable exchange rates, which frees those rates to become even more unstable. This line of thought seems to suggest that fluctuating exchange rates are doing some real harm, by degrading the quality of price signals.

In this third lecture I have argued against the view that we get only as much exchange-rate volatility as we deserve. If financial markets were reliable, exchange rates would be unstable only to the degree that policies were unstable. This would reduce the case for fixed exchange rates to the argument that exchange-rate targets help stabilize and/or coordinate policies—a respectable line of argument, but one that has never been the main action. In fact, the markets have looked a lot more like Ragnar Nurkse's vision than like Milton Friedman's. There is nothing in the experience of the 1980s to support the view that if governments get their policies right, the exchange rate will take care of itself.

Together, these arguments seem to me to have very clear implications for doctrine. Unfortunately, their implications for policy are much less clear.

The doctrinal point is that in the dispute between New England and the Midwest, New England is right. The Midwesterner regards exchange-rate flexibility as unnecessary, because real exchange rates don't need to change and, anyway, nominal prices are flexible. The New Englander thinks that prices are sticky—and she is right. On the other hand, the Midwesterner isn't very worried about flexible rates, because he is sure that speculators will stabilize the rates; the New Englander is concerned that financial markets will be short-sighted and unreliable—and they are. The anxiety-ridden salt-water view of the international monetary system, not the fresh-water confidence that everything will be perfect if the government will only get out of the way, is the doctrinal position supported by the experience of the 1980s.

Unfortunately, this doesn't tell us what to do. We have now concluded that exchange-rate flexibility is useful but dangerous. Now what?

A Prescription for the International Monetary System

My onetime teacher Charles Kindleberger used to tell his students that anyone who spends too much time thinking about the international monetary system ends up going a little mad. What he meant, if I've got it right, is that eventually your desire to find the perfect answer makes you start to think that if only people would adopt your technical proposals, all problems would be solved—that is, you become a bit of a crank. By this measure, I have not yet gone mad, because I do not believe that I can solve all the problems. Indeed, as I just explained, I view the world as full of essentially insoluble problems. The best that one can do is make the tradeoff among problems that seems best in light of the current information.

For most of my professional career, I believed that freely floating exchange rates represented the best system available. The macroeconomic advantages of exchange-rate flexibility, which I reaffirmed in the first of these lectures, seemed clear, and I was strongly influenced by the known failings of international monetary systems in which exchange-rate adjustment is discretionary instead of being left up to the market.

I have now changed my mind. Based on the view I now have of how floating rates work in practice, I am now an advocate of an *eventual* return to a system of more or less fixed rates subject to discretionary adjustment.

This change of mind results from two observations. The first is that the delinking of exchange rates and trade that (as I argued in the second lecture) seems to be occurring as a result of exchange-rate volatility is an argument against allowing such volatility on a routine basis. It seems that exchange-rate adjustment is a little bit like those antibiotics that lose their effectiveness if used too widely, because they lead to the emergence of resistant strains of bacteria. We should avoid a system in which massive exchange-rate changes occur all the time for no very good reason, so that exchange-rate changes will be effective when we need them. The second of these observations, and the theme of the first half of this third lecture, is that financial markets are not to be trusted; they can drive exchange rates far away from a sensible value, doing real harm in the process. This is an argument for government policies that establish a focus for exchange-rate expectations and defend that focus even at the cost of some change in monetary policy. In effect, I am arguing that the exchange rate is too important a price to be left wholly at the mercy of the exchange markets.

In advocating a return to official parities I am quite aware of the problems that adjustable-peg systems are famous for. Once setting the exchange rate becomes government business, there is a strong temptation for governments to try to hold onto rates for too long, and to allow the defense of an excessively high exchange rate to warp macroeconomic policy and trade policy. Also, since governments often try to sustain the unsustainable, central banks offer speculators a one-way option that invites speculative attacks. The Bretton Woods era was by no means a golden age; there have been times since 1973 when the world economy would probably have done worse if countries had tried to defend any fixed set of parities. All I can say is that real exchange rates have gotten further out of line under floating rates than they ever did under fixed rates, and that speculative attacks on currencies seem to happen even without central banks' providing a one-way option.

The most popular proposals for a return to more fixed exchange rates are those that call for "target zones"—reference bands that are, say, ten percentage points wide—rather than rigidly fixed rates. Such proposals are meant to provide a comfortable "halfway house" between fixed and floating rates. There is much to be said for schemes like that proposed by Williamson (1983), but we are fooling ourselves if we imagine that target zones do away with the problems of fixed rates. Indeed, they will function much more like fixed rates than like floating rates. A target zone, if perceived as highly credible, will very nearly fix the exchange rate, because it will give rise to strongly regressive expectations. When the exchange rate is near the top of the band, the market will perceive that the rate has more room to go down than up, so the expected rate of change will be negative; when the rate is near the bottom of the band, the market will perceive that the rate has more room to go up than down, so the expected rate of change will be positive. The result will be to stabilize the exchange rate quite strongly; the promise of future government action will keep exchange rates from moving much even when "fundamentals" (trade balances, price levels, etc.) suggest the desirability of a substantial change in the exchange rate. Conversely, a loss of government credibility will quickly push the exchange rate past the edge of the band. In other words, target zones will present both the temptation to try to sustain the wrong exchange rate and the risk of speculative attack on the target that an unsustainable fixed rate presents.

Thus, I am not very concerned about the technical details. I am now, to my own considerable surprise, an advocate of an eventual return to some kind of adjustable-peg system. This may be easier to achieve if the pegs are fat, and if so I am all for fat pegs.

The key word, however, is *eventual*. There is an extremely difficult transition process ahead, one that makes me unwilling to support any attempt to stabilize parities immediately. That is, my position is that of Saint Augustine: "Oh Lord, make me chaste and continent, but not yet."

Getting from Here to There

There are two problems with any attempt to move to a system of more or less fixed exchange rates: We don't know what the right rates are, and we are not ready for the right rates anyway.

The problem of finding the right rates is one that I have emphasized in this lecture. Between the structural changes that have taken place since we had anything that looked like sustainable rates and the dust cloud that has been thrown up by exchange-rate volatility itself, it is very difficult to make even a plausible guess at the right rates. In particular, the trade numbers are flashing the signal that the dollar needs to decline a lot more, while direct comparisons of costs and prices suggest that it may be nearly there. I have tried to explain why these signals conflict, but nobody can honestly be sure that he knows what weight to put on each signal.

Of course, this will always be true. Even if we get the rates right at some point, a little while later they will be wrong again, requiring some mix of differential inflation and occasional realignment. However, as I will explain in a moment, there is reason to believe that there will be a better opportunity to start from more or less correct rates a few years from now than we have now.

And a time of great uncertainty about rates is not a good time to launch an international monetary reform. Creating such a system will require a major investment of credibility and goodwill—an investment that will be squandered if the system quickly collapses or is forced into such large and frequent realignments that it takes on the appearance of a public-relations exercise rather than a serious change of regime. The unrealistic promises and quick demise of the Louvre accord provided a dress rehearsal for this play; we should be cautious about trying again before we are ready.

In any case, if we were to get the right exchange rates, we would not be ready for them. The main reason is the U.S. budget deficit. The dollar needs ultimately to be at a level at which the United States can run more of less balanced trade, but a quick movement toward such balance with the budget deficit unchecked will threaten a serious overheating of the U.S. economy. Indeed, we may already be set up for this; with the U.S. trade deficit beginning to fall, and with American voters having demonstrated in the presidential primaries that they don't want to hear realism about the budget deficit, it is a fair prediction that the key economic difficulty by the time these lectures are published will be not the persistence of the U.S. trade deficit but the need to cope with the consequences of its shrinkage.

A secondary and counterpart problem is posed by the unwillingness of Germany to expand domestic demand, which means that the shrinkage of the U.S. trade deficit threatens a recession in Europe. This is less serious than the problem of the U.S. budget deficit, since the force of events will probably lead to the right decisions in the end; however, it adds to my belief that we are not ready to institute a formal system of stabilized rates. In effect I am making the implied other point of my first lecture: I emphasized that external adjustment requires getting the exchange rate right as well as redistributing expenditure, but it is also true that it requires redistributing expenditure as well as getting the rate right—and neither the deficit countries nor the surplus countries seem quite ready yet to do what they must.

So what is my proposal? I am not going to propose a complete strategy of benign neglect toward exchange rates. The concerns of central bankers about runaway markets are, as I emphasized, worth taking seriously. However, I think that these concerns can be allayed with very wide zones for the exchange rates (say, from 100 to 150 for the yen and from 1.5 to 2 for the mark), which would provide some assurance that really wild speculative movements would be curbed but which would not tie the rates down to any narrow and almost surely unsustainable band.

Meanwhile, we need to create the preconditions for relatively stable rates. The United States needs to correct its fiscal deficit, and Germany needs to reduce its penchant for self-punishing (and neighbor-punishing) monetary policy. As policies become more stable, we can expect exchange rates to become more stable as well—not as stable as we would like, but sufficiently stable that, as in the 1970s, there will be much less uncertainty than now about what the right rates are. After a few years of a virtuous circle in which stable policies reduce exchange-rate uncertainty and reduced uncertainty makes equilibrium rates more apparent and thus further reduces exchange-rate uncertainty, it could at last be reasonable to expect a grand international monetary conference to produce an agreement with a good chance of lasting long enough to give the new system credibility.

This is not a very inspiring vision, I suppose. It calls for a gradual process of edging up to the starting line for a reformed system, rather than a bold and immediate initiative. And even the initial progress toward that starting line depends on an increased responsibility of public policy that is not evidently forthcoming (that indeed now requires that the winner of the 1988 U.S. election break his campaign promises). So I don't see more stable exchange rates as a quick prospect. But then I warned you: Not being crazy in Kindleberger's sense, I am bad material for an international monetary reformer.

In the end, these lectures are about how to think about exchange-rate policy more than about what to do tomorrow. It is tempting to quote Keynes here and assert that telling people how to think is what really matters in the long run—but I'm not Keynes, and anyway the ebb and flow of intellectual fashion in international monetary economics does not encourage a faith in the power of ideas to do much more than tell people what they want to hear. I have only a more modest hope: that those who came to listen to these lectures found the experience even a fraction as rewarding as I found the giving of them.

Appendix: Diagnosing Speculative Bubbles

A key argument in lecture 3 was that international financial markets cannot be trusted—in particular, that foreign exchange markets sometimes place the exchange rate at levels far from anything that makes sense given the fundamentals. This is a highly controversial view, and one that many economists dislike on principle; my willingness to toss aside the *a priori* assumption of financial-market efficiency is, for better or worse, exceptional.

My conversion to a lack of faith in financial markets was heavily conditioned by the sharp rise of the dollar from mid-1984 to early 1985. That rise, unaccompanied by any obvious news about fundamentals, raised questions in many people's minds about whether the dollar's level "made sense." This is, however, a difficult question to ask in general. One can offer an estimate of what the dollar *should* be worth according to some model and, if that value is exceeded, declare that the market is wrong; but this is a degree of intellectual hubris that few economists (as opposed to financial-market analysts) are prepared to undertake. What we would like is a weaker test—one that does not specify a right value for the dollar, but one that will sound the alarm when the market is clearly enough wrong. In early 1985 I devised what I thought then and still think now is such a test, and it indicated at that point that the market was indeed clearly wrong in the value to which it had driven the dollar. In this appendix I will review that test and what it tells us.

The essence of the test lies in two observations. First, the willingness of international investors to supply capital inflows to a country at some given real interest differential involves an implicit forecast of the future path of the real exchange rate. That is, if foreign investors are willing to put money into U.S. securities when the real interest rate in the United States is 3 percent above that elsewhere, they are implicitly forecasting that the U.S. real exchange rate will not, on average, decline by more than 3 percent per year—otherwise the capital losses on dollar assets would outweigh the higher interest yield. Second, in view of the relationship between the real exchange rate and the trade balance—a relationship that has been questioned, but whose honor I attempted to defend in lecture 1—a forecast of the future path of the exchange rate is also implicitly a forecast of the future path of the trade balance and hence of the accumulation of foreign debt.

Putting these together, we can in principle calculate the forecast path of a country's foreign debt that is implicit in the current exchange rate and interest differential. And we can then ask whether that path is *feasible*. Does debt grow explosively, with a growing burden of interest payments outpacing the slow decline in the trade deficit? If so, the implied forecast path of the exchange rate is not feasible. If debt does not grow explosively—if the growth in interest payments is outrun by an improving trade balance—we can still ask whether the debt peaks at an impossibly high level. There are no hard and fast rules for how much debt is too much, but we can hope to know an impossible debt level when we see one.

If the implicit forecast path is not feasible, then the market's implicit forecast, which supports the current level of the exchange rate, is wrong. In particular, *the currency must decline more rapidly than the market now expects.* This sets us up for a sudden decline at some point. When the market realizes that the exchange rate must decline more rapidly than it thought, the increase in expected capital losses leads to an immediate fall in the currency's value and, hence, a bursting of the bubble.

What I did in early 1985 (Krugman 1985, 1987) was set up a simple algebraic model incorporating these insights, and apply it to the value of the dollar and the interest differential at that point. The warning device immediately flashed the signal that the market was wrong—that the implied debt path for the United States, in view of the value of the dollar and the interest differential, was explosive. Efforts to find a rationale—something the market knew that I didn't—quickly became implausible. The implication was that the market was simply making a massive mistake that could be diagnosed without any special information.

Before turning to the implications of this conclusion, let me present the structure of the algebraic analysis.

Calculating the Market's Implicit Forecast

Consider an economy whose net foreign debt at the end of last year is D_{t-1}, and whose trade deficit this year is B_t. Then if the country pays a nominal interest rate i on its external debt, its debt at the end of this year will be

$$D_t = B_t + (1 + i)D_{t-1}. \tag{A.1}$$

When we consider the growth of debt, of course, it is always important to measure it relative to income—a growth of nominal debt that is outpaced by the growth of nominal income due either to real growth or to inflation should not pose any particular problem. Let us therefore express both debt and trade deficit as ratios to GNP, and use lowercase letters to represent these ratios. Let us also define r as the real interest rate in terms of domestic goods and g as the real rate of growth of the economy. Then a little bit of algebra will show that the growth of the debt-GNP ratio approximately follows the equation

$$d_t = b_t + (1 + r - g)d_{t-1} \tag{A.2}$$

—or, as it will turn out to be convenient to express it,

$$d_t - d_{t-1} = b_t + (r - g)d_{t-1}. \tag{A.3}$$

Equation A.3 implies that if $r > g$ and if a country begins with a net external debt position and a trade deficit, a constant trade deficit will lead to a debt-GNP ratio that not only rises without limit but does so at an accelerating rate. If debt accumulation is not to be runaway, the trade deficit must decline and eventually become a trade surplus large enough to pay the interest on the accumulated debt.

A declining trade deficit will result from a declining exchange rate. What we do is work out the implicit path for foreign debt that results from assuming that the exchange rate declines at the same rate as the real interest differential between the debtor nation and the rest of the world. Let r^* be the foreign real interest rate, and let E_t be the logarithm of the real exchange rate at time t. Then the exchange-rate rule we will use is

$$E_{t+1} - E_t = r^* - r. \tag{A.4}$$

Note that this is *not* the forecast that the economist is making. It is the forecast that the *market* is implicitly making, and we are testing to see if it makes sense.

The trade deficit depends on the real exchange rate. If we assume that the relationship may be approximated by a linear one, we have

$$b_t = a(E_t - \bar{E}), \tag{A.5}$$

where $\bar{E}$ is the real rate at which trade is balanced and where a is the effect of a 1 percent change in the real exchange rate on the trade deficit, measured as a percentage of GNP.

We now have all the elements we need to run our quick test of the feasibility of the market's expectations. Rewriting equation A.3, we have

$$d_t - d_{t-1} = a(E_t - \bar{E}) + (r - g)d_{t-1}. \tag{A.6}$$

Taking first differences, we have

$$\begin{aligned}
(d_{t+1} - d_t) &- (d_t - d_{t-1}) \\
&= a(E_{t+1} - E_t) + (r - g)(d_t - d_{t-1}).
\end{aligned} \tag{A.7}$$

Finally, substituting in the implicit forecast of exchange-rate decline, we have

$$(d_{t+1} - d_t) - (d_t - d_{t-1})$$
$$= a(r^* - r) + (r - g)(d_t - d_{t-1}). \qquad (A.8)$$

This difference equation embodies what we are now calling the market's implicit forecast for the accumulation of external debt.

Testing for Feasibility

The most fundamental requirement for feasibility of the market's forecast is that it not imply an explosive path for foreign debt. It is useful to think of the quantity $d_t - d_{t-1}$ as the current-account deficit adjusted for inflation and debt. If debt is not to grow explosively, this adjusted current-account deficit must sooner or later decline to zero. However, it is immediately apparent from equation A.8 that such a decline will take place only if the right-hand side is initially negative; if it is positive, the adjusted current-account deficit will rise, and that (since the right-hand side is itself increasing in that adjusted deficit) it will keep on rising. Thus, a minimum criterion for feasibility of the market's expectations is that

$$(r - r^*)/(r - g) > (d_t - d_{t-1})/a. \qquad (A.9)$$

But consider what this means. The left-hand side is the real interest differential divided by the interest-growth differential. The right-hand side may be interpreted as the percentage decline in the exchange rate that would be necessary to balance the adjusted current account at the

current level of debt. We may, for short, call this the deviation of the exchange rate from its long-run sustainable
level—bearing in mind that there is nothing inherently
wrong or unreasonable about the exchange rate's sometimes deviating from the level that keeps the debt-GNP
ratio constant. What the inequality says, however, is that
an exchange rate above its long-run sustainable level
"makes sense" only if it is associated with an interest differential large enough to compensate investors for an exchange-rate decline that is sufficiently rapid to prevent
runaway growth in foreign debt.

In early 1985 I suspected that the situation then—a dollar
clearly far above its long-run sustainable level, supported
by only a modest real interest differential—did not make
sense. A rough calculation seems to confirm this insight. I
reproduce here the calculation from Krugman 1987. Using
parameters from the Federal Reserve's MCM model, I estimated that a continuation of the dollar at its level in the
first quarter of 1985 would have led to a current deficit,
excluding interest, of 5.8 percent of GNP (note that lags in
the adjustment of trade to the exchange rate complicate the
calculation here). The parameter a as calculated from
the Federal Reserve's model was 0.1; that is, the deviation
of the exchange rate from its long-run sustainable level was
$0.058/0.1 = 0.58$. Meanwhile, I estimated $r = 0.083$, $r^* =
0.055$, and $g = 0.03$; thus,

$$(r - r^*)/(r - g) = 0.5283.$$

Thus, the calculation for early 1985 suggested that the existing real interest differential was so modest compared
with the dollar's strength that the market was implicitly

forecasting a runaway growth in debt. Since this could not have been right, the dollar was on a speculative bubble.

How Much Debt Is Too Much?

What if the calculation had shown that the path of debt was not runaway? In that case we would still have had to ask whether the peak debt accumulation was reasonable. This situation was actually confronted in Krugman 1985, where the calculation was based on the exchange rates after the dollar had already declined significantly and on deliberately optimistic assumptions about the effect of the dollar's decline on the trade balance. In that calculation it was found that the implied path for U.S. foreign debt was one that would show a rising debt-GNP ratio for more than 20 years and a peak ratio of more than 50 percent of GNP. I argued then that this scenario, with the United States becoming in effect a giant Latin American-level debtor, was not a possible one, and that the market was making a mistake even though its implicit forecast did not imply literally runaway debt.

Why would a large but finite level of foreign debt not be feasible? The answer lies in the *political* incentives such a level of debt would create. As the experience of the debt crisis has shown us, financial obligations of one country to another (whether or not these are explicitly obligations of the debtor country's government) pose problems of enforceability. With the age of gunboat diplomacy in the service of investors long gone, there is no direct police power that can require a country to repay its debts, and hence no clear way for a country to credibly promise to repay. In-

stead, the incentive to repay rests on the indirect consequences of a debt repudiation on a country's reputation,
access to capital markets, trade negotiations, and other po-
tentially important but vague costs of default. Fear of the
consequences of default may induce a country to repay
when a straightforward calculation of measurable impacts
on cash flow would seem to indicate that the country has
more to gain from refusing to pay than from continuing to
service its debt. However, if the debt is large enough, the
certain benefits of default will outweigh the uncertain
costs. More to the point, at a level of debt that is well below
the point at which default becomes likely, investors will
begin to regard it as possible; and their fears of potential
default will impose a limit on the country's further borrowing. This is what happened to the Latin Americans rather
suddenly in 1982.

This ties into the discussion in section 3.1 of the surprisingly limited extent of international capital-market integration, which I attributed to the changes in the political
environment since the prewar era. In 1900 the major capi-
talist powers regarded property rights as sacred, and they
could bully the minor powers into the same opinion (or
seize their customs houses if they disagreed). The sophisticated welfare states of 1988 may still be imperialists in the
eyes of the Third World, but the stark simplicity of those
days is gone, and with it the assurance that allowed British
investors to buy Argentine bonds with the same aplomb
with which they bought domestic debt. As a result, in the
1980s international lending has collapsed, with debtor nations far less heavily indebted relative to income than was
considered perfectly reasonable 80 years earlier.

But what has all this got to do with the United States? To many people the idea of the United States' repudiating its foreign debt seems inconceivable. Yet this is largely because the idea of the United States with a foreign debt of 50 percent of GNP, with interest payments consuming a third of our income from exports, seems inconceivable. As we have seen, however, this is what the market was implicitly forecasting in 1985.

In fact, the very aspects of the United States that make a Latin-style debt crisis seem inconceivable probably reduce the United States' ability to borrow abroad. The United States, because it is less dependent on foreign trade than most other countries, would not be severely hurt by disruption of its foreign trade after a debt default; in any case, because the United States is so large and powerful, it is difficult to imagine other countries' imposing economic retaliation on the United States after a U.S. default on debt. The implication of this, however, is that the United States would be more tempted than other nations to default, because the potential costs would be smaller. As a result, we can expect capital flows to the United States to dry up at the lower level of indebtedness relative to GNP than happens with other countries. This is just the converse of the observation that the countries that seem to be able to run up the largest ratios of foreign debt to GNP are small countries that are heavily dependent on good economic relations with their trading partners, such as Denmark and Ireland.

On this argument, it seems unlikely that the United States would be allowed to run as far into debt as the major Latin debtors. Thus, not only the explosive debt growth that the market was implicitly forecasting in early 1985 but also the transformation into a giant Brazil that the market was forecasting some months later was infeasible.

The Role of Uncertainty

When this analysis was first offered in early 1985, several economists objected to me that the idea of the market's implicit forecast neglected the real uncertainty of market participants about the dollar's future path. They argued that the market did not really anticipate a steady slow decline in the dollar; instead it expected a sharp fall in the dollar at some point, but was unsure about when. This is a good point—but it strengthens, not weakens, the argument that the dollar was at an unreasonably high level.

To see this, consider what the market must believe if it thinks that there is some possibility of a sudden sharp decline in the dollar at any point in time. If investors are still willing to hold dollar assets, it must be because they regard the interest differential net of whatever happens if the dollar does *not* collapse as compensating them for this expected loss. That is, in each year that the dollar does not collapse it must be expected to decline *more slowly* than the interest differential.

The key point now is that there is always a finite possibility that the dollar will go on for any given length of time before it collapses. Therefore, if the market's expectations are to make sense, the path followed by the dollar in the absence of a collapse must itself be feasible. But this path must involve a shallower decline in the exchange rate, a slower decline in the trade deficit, and thus a more rapid accumulation of foreign debt than the path we calculated on the assumption that there is no possibility of a dollar collapse. If the path we calculated in the algebraic treatment above is infeasible, the possibility of a dollar collapse will not make it feasible. If it is feasible, the possibility of a dollar collapse may make it infeasible. In other words, the possibility of a dollar collapse makes it *harder*, not easier, to justify a high dollar for a given interest differential.

What It All Implies

The fact that at the dollar's peak a huge deviation of the exchange rate from its long-run sustainable level was supported by only a modest interest differential was not a secret or an inaccessible piece of information. Indeed, professional forecasters were consistently predicting a future rate of dollar decline that greatly exceeded that interest differential. The willingness of investors to buy dollar-denominated assets despite this did not stem from alternative macroeconomic forecasts. Rather, it seems to have reflected a willingness of the exchange market to simply disregard fundamentals.

Exactly why more people did not declare that the imperial dollar had no clothes is unclear. A casual impression is that many market players did not think about fundamentals at all, while those that did believed that they would be able to get out before the fall.

Bibliography

Dixit, A. 1987a. Entry and Exit Decisions of a Firm under Fluctuating Exchange Rates. Mimeo, Princeton University.

Dixit, A. 1987b. Hysteresis, Import Pricing, and Pass-Through. Mimeo, Princeton University.

Feldstein, M., and C. Horioka. 1980. "Domestic saving and international capital flows." *Economic Journal* 90: 314–329.

Frankel, J., and K. Froot. 1985. "Using survey data to test some standard propositions regarding exchange rate expectations." *American Economic Review* 77: 133–153.

Friedman, M. 1953. "The case for flexible exchange rates." In *Essays in Positive Economics* (University of Chicago Press).

Hooper, P., and C. Mann. 1987. *The U.S. External Deficit: Causes and Persistence.* Federal Reserve Board.

Krugman, P. 1985. "Is the strong dollar sustainable?" In *The U.S. Dollar: Prospects and Policy Options* (Federal Reserve Bank of Kansas City).

Krugman, P. 1987. "Sustainability and the decline of the dollar." In *External Deficits and the Dollar*, ed. R. Bryant, G. Holtham, and P. Hooper (Washington, D.C.: Brookings Institution).

Krugman, P., and R. Baldwin. 1987. *The Persistence of the U.S. Trade Deficit.* Brookings Papers on Economic Activity.

Mann, C. 1987. *After the Fall: The Declining Dollar and Import Prices.* Federal Reserve Board.

Marris, S. 1985. *Deficits and the Dollar: The World Economy at Risk.* Washington: Institute for International Economics.

McKinnon, R. 1984. *An International Standard for Monetary Stabilization.* Washington: Institute for International Economics.

Mundell, R. 1987. A New Deal on Exchange Rates. Paper presented at Japan-U.S. Symposium on Exchange Rates and Macroeconomics, Tokyo.

Nurkse, R. 1944. *International Currency Experience.* League of Nations.

Poterba, J., and L. Summers. 1987. Mean Reversion in Stock Prices: Evidence and Implications. NBER Working Paper 2343.

Williamson, J. 1983. *The Exchange Rate System.* Washington, D.C.: Institute for International Economics.

Index